James Merrill

Twayne's United States Authors Series

Warren French, Editor

Indiana University

TUSAS 427

JAMES MERRILL
Photograph by Thomas Victor

James Merrill

By Ross Labrie
/14
University of British Columbia

Twayne Publishers • Boston

James Merrill

Ross Labrie

Copyright © 1982 by G.K. Hall & Company
All Rights Reserved
Published by Twayne Publishers
A Division of G. K. Hall & Company
70 Lincoln Street
Boston, Massachusetts 02111

Book Production by Marne B. Sultz

Book Design by Barbara Anderson

Printed on permanent/durable acid-free
paper and bound in the United States of
America.

**Library of Congress Cataloging in
Publication Data**

Labrie, Ross.
James Merrill.

(Twayne's United States authors series :
TUSAS 427)
Bibliography: p.157
Includes index.
1. Merrill, James Ingram——Criticism
and interpretation. I. Title. II. Series.
PS3525.E6645Z77 811'.54   82-4750
ISBN 0-8057-7361-4   AACR2

For Ernest and Helen Labrie

Contents

About the Author

Ross Labrie teaches American literature in the English Department at the University of British Columbia. Professor Labrie has published *The Art of Thomas Merton* (Texas Christian University Press, 1979) and *Howard Nemerov* (Twayne, 1980), as well as over a dozen articles on modern American writers, including Henry James, Dorothy Parker, and Joyce Carol Oates. An interview with James Merrill by Professor Labrie was published in the *Arizona Quarterly* in the spring of 1982.

Preface

The presentation of the National Book Award in 1967 to James Merrill's *Nights and Days* brought official recognition to an American poet whose work up to that time had tended to receive unenthusiastic respect. Subsequent awards of the Bollingen Prize, the Pulitzer Prize, and a second National Book Award in the 1970s have confirmed the judgment of the 1967 panel of judges. Moreover, praise in recent years from distinguished scholars like Helen Vendler and David Kalstone has established an honored place for Merrill within the academic community. In addition, his work has now been widely anthologized so that his reputation outside the academic world has also become considerable in the last decade or so.

Merrill's success is not a little ironic since he is one of the most hermetic writers America has produced. His principal subject for much of his career has been a Proustian preoccupation with his own perceptions and with memories of his relationship to his parents, a relationship he has presented in a hundred different lights in both prose and verse. Merrill's ability to make distinguished art out of the quotidian details of his relatively uneventful life has enlarged the possibilities for contemporary writers whose experience lacks the dramatic potential of Confessional poets like Lowell, Berryman, and Plath, or whose social commitment lacks the impassioned drive of poets like Ginsberg and Ferlinghetti. In recent years, with volumes like *Divine Comedies, Mirabell,* and *Scripts for the Pageant,* Merrill has enlarged the scale of introspective poetry by linking man's fate to his ability to re-mythologize his world.

The present volume is the first full-length study of Merrill's poems, fiction, and plays and includes an introductory section on his conception of art. The author wishes to thank James Merrill for his kindness in answering questions about his work both in person and by letter and to express his gratitude to the Social Sciences and Research Council of Canada for the leave fellowship that made the book possible. The author would also like to thank Timothy Murray and

Holly Hall of the Olin Library at Washington University in St. Louis for their generous assistance.

Ross Labrie

University of British Columbia

Chronology

1926   James Ingram Merrill born March 3, New York City, son of Charles E. Merrill and Hellen (Ingram) Merrill. His father was a partner in the large investment firm of Merrill, Lynch, Pierce, Fenner and Beane, and had been one of the founders of Safeway Stores.

1939–1943   Attends the highly rated Lawrenceville prep school near Princeton, New Jersey.

1942   *Jim's Book: A Collection of Poems and Short Stories* (privately printed).

1943   Enters Amherst College.

1944–1945   Private, United States Army.

1946   *The Black Swan* (poems, privately printed).

1947   B.A., *summa cum laude,* from Amherst.

1948–1949   Instructor, Bard College.

1950   Extended trip to Europe. Travels to Europe and Asia continue through the 1950s.

1951   *First Poems.* Receives the Harriet Monroe Memorial Prize.

1953   *The Bait,* Merrill's first play, produced in New York.

1954   *Short Stories* (poems). Merrill and David Jackson take up temporary residence in Stonington, Connecticut, on Long Island Sound. They will live there permanently after 1956.

1955–1956   Teaches in the English Department at Amherst. Merrill's second play, *The Immortal Husband,* is successfully produced in New York.

1957   *The Seraglio* (novel).

1958   Lengthy visit to the southwestern states in the winter of 1958.

1959 *The Country of a Thousand Years of Peace,* poems. Begins living in Greece for part of each year.

1961 *Selected Poems.* First edition of his poems in Great Britain.

1962 *Water Street* (poems).

1965 *The (Diblos) Notebook* (novel, nominated for the National Book Award).

1966 *Nights and Days* (poems). Receives the National Book Award.

1967 Gives a poetry workshop at the University of Wisconsin, Madison.

1968 D.Litt., Amherst College.

1969 *The Fire Screen,* poems. Guest lecturer at Washington University, St. Louis. Second visit to Southwest.

1971 Elected to the National Institute of Arts and Letters.

1972 *Braving the Elements* (poems). Awarded the Bollingen Prize.

1974 *The Yellow Pages* (poems).

1976 *Divine Comedies* (poems). Awarded the Pulitzer Prize.

1978 *Mirabell: Books of Number* (poem). Receives the National Book Award.

1980 *Scripts for the Pageant* (poem).

Chapter One

Merrill's Life and Art

Biographical Background

James Merrill's boyhood was spent in affluent surroundings on Long Island and in Palm Beach, Florida. His father, who is vividly characterized in Merrill's novel *The Seraglio,* controlled what was to become one of the largest investment firms in the world. Merrill's mother, Hellen Ingram, was Charles Merrill's second wife, and while still a boy, Merrill was to witness the collapse of his parents' marriage as his father moved on to a third (1937–38), an episode that was to sink deeply into his poetry. In an unpublished sketch written in recollection of that period of his life he has written wryly about the "finale of a marriage, scored as it is for full orchestra complete with triangle, child soloist, and massed legal strings." In the same sketch he recalls the momentous effect on his life caused by the withdrawal of his father whose absence from the household seemed to erase "all recollection of a masculine element."[1] On the whole, Merrill has said that he "didn't very much care" for the world as seen through his parents' eyes, "and yet since I didn't know very many other worlds—I couldn't imagine which one I would fit into."[2] In spite of Merrill's reservations about having a tycoon for a father, Charles Merrill's wealth was to make his son financially independent for the rest of his life.

Merrill attended the private Lawrenceville School near Princeton, New Jersey, where he began to write poems largely due to his friendship with fellow student Frederick Buechner, who was to become an author of note himself (his first novel, *A Long Day's Dying,* 1950, was especially well received). Merrill's *First Poems* are dedicated to him. Merrill and Buechner managed the school magazine, the *Lit.,* in the early 1940s in which Merrill published some narrative sketches and poems. In 1942 he published *Jim's Book,* a collection of poems and short stories that is characteristic of the sort of writing he was doing at this time.

In 1943 Merrill enrolled at Amherst College, an unusual choice for a Lawrenceville graduate, most of whom went on to Princeton. The reason was that Merrill's father had gone to Amherst and wanted his son to follow him there. Though Amherst contributed greatly to the thoroughness of Merrill's intellectual background, it did not make an effort in the mid-1940s to introduce its students to contemporary writers. Merrill recalls that no one "ever taught the works of a living poet—except Frost,"[3] who was associated with Amherst. Moreover, according to Merrill, Kimon Friar, not a regular member of the faculty, singlehandedly provided support for aspiring writers. At Amherst, however, Merrill encountered the work of Proust, who was to become a seminal influence on his own writing. The study of the French author proceeded under the tutelage of Reuben Brower. Although Merrill's studies at Amherst were interrupted by a two-year stint in the army, they were productive years. He played the title role in Cocteau's *Orphée* and had his own unpublished play "The Birthday" produced there as well. In this period also some of his first offerings were accepted by *Poetry* magazine.

After Amherst Merrill set out on his own, dividing his time between apartment living in New York and overseas travel. In an unpublished sketch written in 1948, he describes a cocktail party attended by luminaries like Edith Sitwell, W. H. Auden, Stephen Spender, William Carlos Williams, Marianne Moore, Elizabeth Bishop, and John Berryman. His incisive drawing of Edith Sitwell is especially memorable: "The mouth was large, the eyes, though splendidly socketed, small and, perhaps because of the nose's prominence, appearing close together as though magnetized by what kept them apart. Colorless and hairless was the entire face—only a suggestion of thin, beige hair at the turban's edge. The expression was one of considerable malignity; the manner was kindness and the sort of restraint in which there is nothing to hold back, in which the social utterance is of the same purity or control as the big poetic one."[4] The passage is an early indication of Merrill's deftness in characterization, and in fact he had already begun work on his novel *The Seraglio* in the late 1940s. Because of the intellectual and social stimulation that accompanied living in New York, however, he found that he couldn't do the writing that he wanted to do: "I guess I have to be in a place," he observed later, "where there's nothing to do but work."[5]

The years of travel in the 1940s and 1950s led Merrill into some formative relationships. He befriended a young Dutch poet, Hans Lodeizen, who died tragically of leukemia in Lausanne, Switzerland, in 1950. *The Country of a Thousand Years of Peace* (1958) was dedicated to Lodeizen, and he figures in Merrill's trilogy of divine comedies. Merrill's mixing with people of other cultures had the effect of confirming his felt identity as a sort of Jamesian cosmopolite: "I felt very American when I was living abroad, perhaps in the sense of a Jamesian American, and felt a bit displaced, by the same token, when I would come back here."[6] In 1953 he met David Jackson, with whom he has lived more or less continuously since. Jackson, who was born in South Dakota in 1922, had attended the University of California in Los Angeles to study music. He subsequently took up the study of languages in Europe and then creative writing at the University of Denver. Although Jackson has not published a great deal, his short story "The English Gardens" was picked as one of the O. Henry prize stories for 1962. He was married to the painter Doris Jackson and living in New York when Merrill met him in the 1950s.

Merrill's acceptance of his homosexuality had been painfully if resolutely arrived at in his adolescent years. He recalls his parents' unhappiness about the subject: "They had a clear idea of what I should turn out to be, sexually, and I could see that I was going to disappoint them."[7] He dealt in passing with the theme of the loneliness of the homosexual in writing about Proust for his graduating essay at Amherst. In the poems and novels of the 1950s and 1960s he touches on homosexual relationships, but often masks these relationships by referring to the beloved as a genderless "you." By the 1970s the wraps were off, and in the divine comedies Merrill depicts homosexual activity with witty candor and verve.

The move to the old seaport town of Stonington, Connecticut, with David Jackson, first in 1954 and then for good in 1956, had far-reaching consequences for a poet like Merrill, whose art is autobiographical. Stonington is an isolated town, the easternmost on Connecticut's coast. Its attractive, pillored, white houses and buildings with their star decks and cupolas handsomely preserved the period of Greek revival in American architecture. Merrill and Jackson took up residence on the main street of the town in apartments that overlooked the Sound. In unpublished notes Merrill recalls the way Stonington first appeared to him in 1954: "Self-contained, elongated, fringed with docks, it had the reassuring air of a toy Manhattan. Its one skyscraper, the Baptist Church tower—overlooking a concentration of shops and houses neatly painted round a tiny Central Park—saw eye to eye with the last of the original fine elms that had once lined Main Street."[8] While loyal to this day to the impulse that led to the move to Stonington, Merrill's view of the town has inevitably lost its freshness. In *Mirabell* (1978), for example, small-town life is summed up in words that Sinclair Lewis might have chosen:

> Largely a state of mind, a medium
> Wherein suspended, microscopic figments
> —Boredom, malice, curiosity—
> Catch a steadily more revealing light.(3)[9]

Perhaps because of the stability offered by Stonington Merrill pursued travel in the 1950s with a passion greater than ever. A note attached to a package containing the revisions of one of his poems advised the postmaster to "Please return, if found, to: James Merrill, 107 Water St. Stonington, Conn. or: 950 1st Ave. New York City or: Pension Biederstein Munich (Germany) or: American Express Athens (Greece)." Some of the important journeys were within the United States, like the trip to the Southwest. He spent three months in Santa Fe in the winter of 1958, and returned there for three more months in the fall of 1969. The area haunted his imagination. An even more important journey, however, brought Merrill and Jackson to Greece. In 1959 they moved into a house in Athens across from a pine-covered hill and subsequently divided their time between Stonington and Athens until the late 1970s when they began to winter in Key West, Florida.

The house in Athens served as the occasion for many of Merrill's poems. Greece offered him a longed-for release from American culture and a second identity. He began going to Greece, he remembers, "very much in the spirit of one who embarks upon a double life."[10] He formed new and rewarding relationships in Greece, such as that with the Greek novelist Vassilis Vassilikos. While in Greece he tended to avoid Americans abroad. "In a city like Athens, a few literary Americans inevitably turn up," he once said, "but I don't see them, not much, partly because they are literary and partly because they are American."[11] Merrill relished the anonymity of living in Greece. He spoke a demotic Greek, which fortuitously led to a broader contact with people than was possible in America. Furthermore, in accepting the National Book Award for *Nights and Days* in 1967, he spoke of the purifying effect that being immersed in a foreign language for part of each year had on his use of English. The situation was a "curious, possibly a dangerous, luxury," he pointed out, "but it has borne fruit of a sort."[12] The matter went beyond linguistics to the very way in which he found he perceived others: "It's because of the language barrier—when you can't ascertain the full range of people's motives and feelings, they are simplified in a sense."[13]

Merrill valued as well the simplicity of Greek life. The country seemed to him to be a "world on a surprisingly small human scale compared to the great American world of business, technology and political machines."[14] Among other things, the simplicity brought him into contact with the intimate relationship in Greece between art, myth, and experience: "I have heard a mother advise her child to tell its bad dream to the lighted bulb hanging from a kitchen ceiling, and for the same reason that Clytemnestra, in one of the old plays, tells hers to the sun. For while the ancient glory may have grown dim and prosaic, many forms of it are still intact."[15] Furthermore, Merrill found himself attracted to Greek myth and literature, from Plato to the moderns, not least perhaps because—as a recent commentator has put it—"it is only in Greece that the homosexual may find a culture in which he might have had a place and whose literature speaks directly to his own sexual experience."[16] In particular he has written about and to some extent identified with the life and work of Constantine Cavafy, the homosexual poet who lived and wrote in the Greek section of Alexandria around 1900.

Literary Influences

There was much in Cavafy's life for Merrill to identify with. Cavafy's father died when he was seven, paralleling Merrill's loss of his father through his parents' divorce when he was eleven. In addition, Merrill has identified with Cavafy's open acceptance of his homosexuality, his "refusal to be a husband and father."[17] Moreover, Cavafy wrote about the everyday details of his life, a pattern that was to appeal to Merrill. The most formidable influence on Merrill's writing, however, was undoubtedly Proust, who also adapted his writing to the modest scale of everyday life. Merrill felt indebted to Proust for having shown that there was "nothing too commonplace or too trivial which once seen as a phenomenon either of light or of social behaviour couldn't be dwelt on in perfect seriousness."[18] Like Merrill, Proust came from a wealthy background, was homosexual, apolitical, and avoided becoming entrapped by intellectual systems.

Merrill was also greatly influenced by the poetry of Wallace Stevens, whom he began to read on his own at Amherst. Among contemporary poets, Stevens "was the one who most appealed to me. I loved the vocabulary, where he mixed the very gaudiest words with the grandest philosophical terms as if they were on a par with each other. You could throw off a philosophical term the way you might name a color to get texture and a certain dimension."[19] What Merrill liked especially about Stevens was that his virtuosity in diction did not obscure the sense of his having "had a private life."[20] Yeats was another important influence. In a letter to the author Merrill recalls that "Yeats must have meant a great deal to me. I tried to sound like him (in poems) around the time I graduated."[21] Apart from the evident influence of Yeats on volumes like *The Black Swan* (1946) and *First Poems* (1951), Merrill's recent trilogy (*Divine Comedies,* 1976, *Mirabell,* 1978, and *Scripts for the Pageant,* 1980) reveals a Yeatsian influence, particularly by Yeats's long, cosmological poem, *A Vision.* In acknowledgment of their place in his life and art both Yeats and W. H. Auden show up in parts of Merrill's trilogy. He had read Auden's *The Sea and the Mirror* and *For the Time Being* when he was in the army in the mid-1940s, and was "dazzled" by Auden's "range of forms."[22] If he was attracted by Yeats's rhetorical splendor, he was also impressed by Auden's tonal ironies. He became friends with Auden after he began going to Greece regularly in the late 1950s.

Henry James was another influence whom Merrill has acknowledged, particularly on his novels. Merrill's elongated narrative style, sustained analyses of consciousness, and acceptance of the final merging of the good and the beautiful are all in accord with James. While he admires James "very, very much," however, he feels that the great novelist was restricted to some extent by his elaborate plots: "Because the overlying fiction was not that of a single life as in Proust, he had to taper and shape things."[23] For a similar reason, while he admires the achievement of T. S. Eliot, he is not enthusiastic about Eliot's poetry, which seems to him to have placed a "whole civilization under glass."[24]

Other influences include Rilke, who, Merrill has said, "helps you with suffering, especially in your adolescence,"[25] and Hart Crane. Merrill is attracted to Crane's "clotted" type of writing, which through its verbal density and complexity produces poetry that "resists the intelligence almost successfully, as Stevens said."[26] Other contemporaries whom Merrill has emulated in one way or another include Mallarmé, Valéry, Gertrude Stein, Cocteau, Nabokov, Elizabeth Bishop, Robert Lowell, John Berryman, and Elinor Wylie ("the most magical rhyming we've ever had").[27] Of Lowell, Berryman, and Bishop he wrote in his notes in the 1960s: "On bad days the three of them can be felt as having licked the platter clean."[28] Classical writers whose influence Merrill has acknowledged include Pope (Merrill's patron in *Divine Comedies* is a nineteenth-century editor of Pope), Byron, Blake, Keats, and Donne.[29]

Merrill's Distrust of Ideas

Merrill has expressed an unvarying hostility throughout his career to those who employ poetry for social comment. The poetry of protest, he observed in unpublished notes written during the 1960s, is no less nor more interesting than the sermons and hymns it replaces in the lives of the public. Apart from this sort of objection, however, Merrill has frequently felt alienated from ideas in themselves. Sometimes this alienation took the form of a sense of inadequacy, as in a notebook entry from the early 1950s in which he regretted that, although he had ideas enough, he found himself either unable or unwilling to pursue the "development of an idea."[30] The problem was not one of adequacy, though, since Merrill's later poetry reflects a lucid aptitude for handling sophisticated ideas. The difficulty was essentially one of attitude, as can be seen in *Scripts for the Pageant* where he admits his "chronic shyness / Vis-à-vis 'ideas'—."[31]

Merrill's alienation from ideas goes deeper than attitudinizing, though. In "The Book of Ephraim" in *Divine Comedies* he paraphrases an observation T. S. Eliot once made about Henry James in which Eliot argued that James had a mind so fine that "no idea violates" it (58).[32] Although Merrill does not go further into Eliot's remarks, it is worthwhile citing the following additional comment by Eliot: "James in his novels is like the best French critics in maintaining a point of view, a viewpoint untouched by the parasite idea. He is the most intelligent man of his generation."[33] Eliot's view that one could be extremely intelligent without succumbing to the entrapment of ideas is one of Merrill's deepest convictions. Ironically, this is one reason why he doesn't much care for Eliot's poetry: "We all have our limits. I draw the line at politics or hippies. I'd rather present the world through, say, a character's intelligence or lack of it than through any sort of sociological prism. It's perhaps why I side with Stevens over Eliot. I don't care much about generalizing; it's unavoidable to begin with."[34]

Merrill's distrust of ideas is echoed in the writings of Francis Ponge, one of the few authors he has chosen to write about. He quotes Ponge as saying: "If ideas disappoint me, give me no pleasure, it is because I offer them my approval too easily, seeing how they solicit it, are only made for that."[35] Merrill's skepticism about ideas is based on their seduction of the mind from its more demanding state of idea-less awareness. He is attracted in turn to ideas when they are part of a living context of some sort which gives them depth and substance. Quoting William Carlos Williams's famous maxim, Merrill quips: "No thoughts, then, but in things? True enough, so long as the notorious phrase argues not for the suppression of thought but for its oneness with whatever in the world—pine woods, spider, cigarette—gave rise to it." He adds that a "thought is after all a thing of sorts. Its density, color, weight, etc. vary according to the thinker, to the symbols at his command, or at whose command he thinks. One would hardly care so much for language if this were not the case." He concludes: "Thoughts and things need to be the best of friends."[36]

One of the characteristic ways in which Merrill "thinks" in his poems is through the use of overtones, which he regards as intermediate between thought and things. He dislikes the sort of commentary that attempts to extract abstract statements of meaning from a literary work even if this is endemic to literary criticism. As a result he has written very little criticism, and has avoided the temptation, commonly acceded to by his contemporaries, to set forth a poetics based upon his own practice. The issuance of abstract statements of meaning about a work of art, Merrill believes, inevitably involves the "sacrifice of overtones, whether for the sake of a more concrete image or of a more purified idea."[37] Thus, in expressing his own position as an artist on one occasion, he drolly illustrated the importance of overtone: "I guess I'm an arch-conservative. More arch than conservative, I'm sometimes made to feel."[38]

Along with his fondness for overtones Merrill perceives manners as a refined merging of thought and thing. On one occasion he paraphrased Marianne Moore in order to describe his view of manners observing that, having a "perfect contempt for them, one discovers in them after all a place for the genuine."[39] Addressing himself with unusual solemnity to the relationship between manners and ideas, he commented that manners provide a "framework all the nicer for being more fallible, more hospitable to irony, self-expression, self-contradiction, than many a philosophical or sociological system. Manners for me are the touch of nature, an artifice in the very bloodstream."[40] For Merrill the manners of the writer are a profound and visible part of his writing whether he realizes it or not. Proust's writing succeeds, therefore, because of his "extreme courtesy towards the reader, the voice explaining at once formally and intimately."[41] Merrill's remarks about Proust could easily be applied to his own writings.

Another and more curious intermediary between thought and thing is belief. Although Merrill finds formal religion dull and generally unappealing, he has gravitated increasingly toward the occult both in his life and in poems. His interest in spiritualism and in reincarnation, which are highly conspicuous in his recent poetry, can be traced back to the mid-1950s, showing up in *The Seraglio* (1957), for example. Merrill has confided that the attractiveness of this sort of belief is that it is "very fruitful" and that it "does wonders in a way for the way you live."[42] Belief, or at least the kinds of beliefs illustrated in his poems, may in Merrill's view have little objective value, but he contends that these beliefs have enriched his life and art immeasurably in the past twenty-five years. What matters most to Merrill is not the philosophical certitude of ideas but rather their effect on life, which in his case includes, preeminently, his art.

Merrill's View of Art

Since Merrill has done little expository writing, his view of art must be culled for the most part from scattered observations to interviewers and from unpublished notes. One of his most strongly held convictions about art is that it should, as Ponge said, give "pleasure to the human mind."[43] Furthermore, art nourishes the spirit by keeping it simultaneously in contact both with the physical and the metaphysical: "Any word can lead you from the kitchen-garden into really inhuman depths—if there are any of those left nowadays."[44] The potency of art in Merrill's view is especially apparent in this age in which the patterns of beauty and meaning provided by the artist have supplanted the structures of order and significance previously provided by religion.

The artist swallows history in order to clarify its significance as a framework of behavior and value.[45] He in turn goes on to create history. Merrill felt the truth of this on traveling through the Greek countryside: "I have heard my host in a remote farmhouse tell Aesop's fables as if he had made them up; that they had made *him* up was closer to the truth."[46] For Merrill the poet is a "man choosing the words he lives by."[47] This choosing results in among other things the creation of a "language within a language," as he put it in notes written in 1967.[48] He pictures the writer as setting out for a particular place or seeking a particular experience in the "hopes of finding something to write about. Then you have not simply imitated or recollected experience, but experience in the light of a projected emotion, like a beam into which what you encounter will seem to have strayed. The poem and its occasion will have created one another."[49] Merrill illustrates his view of composition by referring to poems like "Yánnina" in *Divine Comedies,* which grew out of a much anticipated visit to a legendary place. In addition, he has supplied a highly imaginative impression of what he means by "projected emotion" in his short story "Peru: The Landscape Game," which came out in 1971.

Merrill's exposure to music and painting throughout his life has naturally influenced his view of literary art: "Certainly I cared about music long before I cared about literature." When he was eleven years old, he recalled in the same interview, he began being taken to the opera in New York, and he recalls the heightened feelings generated by the music, feelings that "could be expressed without any particular attention to words."[50] The impact of music on his poetry has been extensive. On one occasion he told an interviewer that whenever he reaches an impasse while working on a poem, he tends to "imagine an analogy with musical form."[51] Music gave him the "sound of sheer feeling," which in moments "worth dreaming about" united seamlessly with "verbal sense."[52]

Merrill's manuscripts are filled with pencil sketches of people. "The writer will always envy the painter," he wrote in an essay on Corot published in 1960 "for having learned to pay close attention to appearances."[53] For Merrill the careful observation of particulars is as indispensable an aspect of art as the contemplative uses to which these particulars are put, and few contemporary writers have an acuteness of observation to equal his; inevitably, Proust is the exception who comes to mind. Whatever the art, though, the work that is most satisfying to Merrill is that which reflects the "scale of a human life," as he put it in praising the poetry of Elizabeth Bishop. In her work, he added, there was "no oracular amplification, she doesn't go about on stilts to make her vision wider."[54] Similarly, in an early review of the poet, Robert Bagg, Merrill appreciated Bagg's vivid account of his life making the reader glad that Bagg had had the experiences described. He especially valued Bagg's "clear hold on the commonplace," the daily flow of life.[55]

Writing is quintessentially for Merrill an act of discovery, the discovery above all of what he really thinks and feels or really did think and feel at selected moments in his past. An ironic and fruitful result of the artist's total immersion in his own autobiography is that he can produce, without necessarily trying to do so, an "excellent likeness of the universe."[56] Because writing involves a discovery about what he thinks and feels, Merrill once again has little sympathy with writers who use their poems to disseminate ideas and attitudes. The effect of this sort of thing, he believes, is inevitably ephemeral: "The trouble with overtly political or social writing is that when the tide of feeling goes out the language begins to stink."[57]

As one who is generally thought to be an elitist poet, Merrill appreciates popular art more than one might expect: "Popular art, in a society without ritual," he told a group of students in 1969, "can only be that which entertains, is consumed, and is replaced at once by the next thing. Its admirers include to a man, us aesthetes. That the admiration isn't mutual needn't bother anyone. Some will always have a more complex emotional or intellectual life than others, which a more complex art will be called upon to nourish."[58] Thus, while affirming his own interest in popular art, Merrill concedes that his own writing will appeal to the few: "Think what one has to *do* to get a mass audience. I'd rather have one perfect reader. Why dynamite the pond in order to catch that single silver carp? Better to find a bait that only the carp will take."[59] Although Merrill's tone tends to be generous and playful, open to any reader who will understand and enjoy him, he is not, after all, concerned with depicting most people's minds or most people's lives; in this sense at least he is unashamedly, cheerfully elitist.

Merrill's Impressionism

The chief influence upon Merrill was Proust, whom he regarded as essentially an Impressionist. His ideas about both Proust and Impressionism are contained in a lengthy, unpublished essay he wrote under the direction of Reuben Brower in his final academic year at Amherst, 1946–47. What Merrill says about Proust foreshadows his own work, and thus amounts to an oblique statement about his intentions as an artist. The Impressionist begins either in painting or writing, Merrill wrote, with the assumption that the true existence of an individual lies in his mental processes rather than in the external incidents of his life. Merrill concedes the indissoluble mystery of the external world stressing that objects can only be known through a tentative grasp of shifting sensations. Thus, Impressionist art necessarily mirrors the individual temperament of the artist, who attempts to fix sensations in a momentary illusion of stability and order while inwardly conceding that reality is an endless state of flux whose complexity surpasses the mind's power to deal definitively with it.

The Impressionist fixes sensation by concentrating on the atmosphere surrounding the subject rather than directly on the subject itself. As Merrill later wrote in *Mirabell*: "Not for nothing had the Impressionists / Put subject-matter in its place, a mere / Pretext for iridescent atmosphere" (15). In this light setting becomes crucial: "You hardly ever need to *state* your feelings. The point is to feel and keep the eyes open. Then what you feel is expressed, is mimed back at you by the scene. A room, a landscape. I'd go a step further. We don't *know* what we feel until we see it distanced by this kind of translation."[60] Merrill believes that the generation of an atmosphere that momentarily stabilizes shifting sensations is accomplished particularly through attention to light and color, light being the medium through which color is revealed. The Impressionists came to realize that the "sensuous experience of an object was infinitely variable, depending on the light upon it and other objects around it."[61] The application of this principle to Merrill's own art, from the early still-life poems through to the lyric interludes in the trilogy of divine comedies, is apparent. In addition to the use of light, though, Merrill sees Proust as modifying atmosphere through the use of music, a technique that is also apparent in his own work with its reliance on musical structuring and its meticulous attention to sound.

In addition to creating atmosphere, the Impressionist evoked the illusion of fixed sensations by means of metaphor. The value of metaphor for Merrill lies in its ability both to accommodate the artist's subjectivism and to evoke the illusion of a "personal reality" that is accessible to others. Such an evocation involves the sifting of memory where sensations are stored and where experiences are mingled mysteriously. In this way memory manufactures metaphors within the bloodstream, as it were, even before the artist sets about synthesizing. Mind and memory, instinctively and unconsciously, perceive the analogies between things, giving rise to patterns of order and continuity. In searching his memory, the artist discovers these analogies, to which he adds others which occur to him in composition, and thus gets a glimmering of the unfolding story that is himself. Therefore, through metaphor what is "unknown may be known through analogy, as Einstein is said to have taught a blind man what 'white' is by letting him feel the neck of a swan."

Merrill liked the way Proust delayed the reader's discovery of the full meanings or even the essential meanings of his metaphors so that the reader could respond emotionally to the metaphors before the mind explained them away. Merrill uses the same delaying technique in many of his poems, often sailing into the poem's dramatic perplexities (as in "Maisie" in *Nights and Days* or "Flèche d'Or" in *Braving the Elements*) before the reader has a very clear idea of what the poem is about. Thus, at least some of the obscurity attributed to Merrill can be understood in the light of the strategy he has adopted for his poems. His syntax, which is often elongated and occasionally impenetrable, is an example. He praised the "momentary ambiguity" of Proust's depiction of experience, which he saw as "reproduced in, if not created by, his syntax." He liked such syntactical ambiguity for its ability to mark the intersection between the present moment with its particular stimuli and whatever ghosts in the memory are evoked by those same stimuli. This sort of suspended juxtaposition involving intersecting images of present and past is *the* characteristic situation in Merrill's poems.

Similarly, for Merrill syntax is the vehicle by which the poet can portray the impact of time on experience, a use of space to suggest time. He admired the syntactical unfolding of Proust's symbols which he saw as operating neither in time nor space but in a "dimension of space-time in which both are interdependent." The interfusion of space and time is ubiquitous in Merrill's work, and is especially noticeable in poems like "An Urban Convalescence" in *Water Street* and "The Thousand and Second Night" in *Nights and Days*. In the state of suspended awareness created by Impressionist art, the mind gravitates toward and grapples with the suspended elements of the painting or poem without mastering them, which in the case of a literary work meant not being reduced to abstract statement. Thus, speaking of Proust's *Remembrance of Things Past,* Merrill cautions that we must resist the temptation to take the novelistic sequence as an "image for Something Else, a disconcerting abstraction such as Life or Change; developing on our own part an enormous metaphor in which we would relate our lives and perceptions to Proust's life and perceptions. But this we must not do; or if we must, we should not risk talking about it."

Finally, for Merrill, Impressionism and its agent, metaphor, are of use to the artist not only in allowing him to discover his identity in the retrospective resonance of the present moment but as a palliative for suffering. This kind of art becomes a "way of making pain bearable" since it compels the artist to yield to the fact that in the "very act of expressing reality, his method of expression requires that the expression itself be the only reality." Even though autobiographical writers like Proust and Merrill focus on their own loneliness and pain, the very act of tapping the memory for significant analogies in experience in order to turn these into art is so engrossing and triumphant a process that its satisfactions replace the pain. Furthermore, by analogically linking various images of experience the artist dilutes the unhappy ones by relating them to those which are either happy or at least not unhappy. Little wonder that such a view of art is attractive to Merrill, who often seems to find the solace in writing about his life that he has missed in living it.

A Formal Art

Without meaning to crusade for formalism in art, Merrill accepts the description of himself as a formalist. He recalls having unsuccessfully attempted on various occasions to experiment with freer forms than those he was used to: "Even when I sort of slyly thought of changing to irregular line lengths I always found some way to justify them, by secret scanning and rhyme."[62] Characteristically, he bristled at a translation of Cavafy's poem "Days of 1908" because the translator did not imitate Cavafy's balance of masculine and feminine line endings, which he believes were the poem's "secret power."[63] His own endless revisions of his poems bear witness to his sense of the crucial effects of apparently slight alterations in sound and rhythm. His passion for revision, which he has called the "one dependable pleasure in the whole process" of writing, and his enthusiasm for formal art in general stem from his sense that words "aren't that meaningful in themselves."[64]

Thus, the artist should refrain from serving "uncooked" his "bloody tranche de vie," as Merrill put it in *Scripts for the Pageant* (214). The most exquisite poem in Merrill's view is that in which form is so seamlessly a part of its content that the reader cannot and does not wish to extract a residue of meaning. In Merrill's poem "Marsyas," the superior poet is the one who "Inflicted so much music on the lyre / That no one could have told you what he sang" (50).[65] Similarly, form permits the reconciling of the obdurate dualities that the artist works with: "Words and silence, things and thoughts, excitation and de-tumescence: no opposites but brought into peaceful coexistence."[66] Through a careful attention to form, therefore, the writer turns "iron" into "sunlight" (*Scripts,* 214). An amusing fact for the formal poet, Merrill points out, is that so few readers retain a knowledge of classical poetic conventions that traditional verse forms may soon be mistaken for something new and "read with appropriate cries of delight."[67] While he has a considerable respect for innovation, as his novel *The (Diblos) Notebook* emphatically demonstrates, Merrill is impatient with those writers who proclaim their experimentalism: "People who talk

about experimentation sound as if they thought poets set out deliberately to experiment, when in fact they haven't: they've simply recognized afterwards the newness of what they've done."[68]

While avoiding association with any particular school of poetry,
Merrill feels a kinship with those writers who go in for word play. He
identifies with poets who use English in its "billiard-table sense—
words that have been set spinning against their own gravity" so as to
liberate them from the torpor of "today's headlines or editorial page."[69]
Hence, Merrill's affection for the pun, whose use he feels is especially
appropriate in contemporary writing: "A culture without Greek or
Latin or Anglo-Saxon goes off the gold standard. How to draw upon the
treasure? At once representing and parodying our vital wealth, the
lightweight crackle of word-play would retain no little transactional
power in the right hands." Acutely aware of its notoriety, Merrill
nevertheless defends the pun on the basis that, like the Freudian slip, it
betrays the "hidden wish of words." The poet discovers this hidden
wish in words by allowing them free play, even at the risk of censure.[70]

Few contemporary poets have paid the attention to tone and voice
that Merrill has: "I notice voice a good deal more in metrical poetry.
The line lends itself to shifts of emphasis. If Frost had written free verse,
I don't think we'd have heard as much of the voice in it."[71] Merrill's
response to other writers typically involves his reaction to their tone, as
in his view that Elizabeth Bishop's poems were more "wryly radiant,
more touching, more unaffectedly intelligent than any written in our
lifetime."[72] Merrill's use of tone often involves subtle modulations that
can produce ambiguity. This is especially the case in his divine comedies, but it is true of all of his writings. Merrill's rejoinder to readers
who are uncertain about his seriousness is: "Aren't we used by now to
the light poem that has dark touches and the serious poem shot through
with lighter ones?"[73] The matter is partly one of emotional rhythm;
Merrill wants to avoid either a sustained heaviness or lightness. As well,
though, he often wants to stress the unexpected value of the inessential,
and conversely to satirize the gravity that conventionally surrounds
issues like politics or religion.

Merrill not only uses language with freshness and virtuosity; he also
invites the reader to notice and delight in the artistic illusions projected. He himself has acknowledged the pleasure he has received in

gazing at the transparent and intricate artifices constructed by writers like Nabokov and Ponge. His instinct to reveal his stagecraft can be seen in the various layers of novelistic construction laid out in *The (Diblos) Notebook* as well as in the many genial asides in which he suddenly breaches the surface of his poems in order to consider their progress. His primary intent as a writer, on these occasions and elsewhere, has always been to charm his reader. [74]

Chapter Two
Plays

The Bait

In retrospect Merrill has said that his experience as a dramatist in the 1950s left him on "fresh terms with language," having freed him from the necessity of always having to speak in his own voice.[1] His one-act play *The Bait* was performed off Broadway by the Artists' Theatre group in 1953 and was subsequently aired on the BBC in England in 1955. Under the direction of Herbert Machiz the Artists' Theatre attempted to revive poetic drama in an effort to offer an alternative to Naturalism. Other playwrights in the group included John Ashbery and Frank O'Hara.

The Bait focuses introspectively on the lives of four affluent, well-traveled, rather jaded American sophisticates. They include Julie, her husband, Charles, her brother, Gilbert, and her fiancé, John. The action shuttles between the two principal settings, Venice and the Caribbean, and between past and present. The three men in the play vie for Julie's love, but it is clear that her brother, Gilbert, a fastidious aesthete reminiscent of Gilbert Osmond in Henry James's *Portrait of a Lady*, has the greatest influence on her. The pivotal action occurs in a flashback in which Julie, Gilbert, and Charles are on a fishing trip over the Gulf Stream. In an attempt to show his own healthy freedom from the clannish, lifelong consciousness shared by Gilbert and Julie, Charles decides to attach himself to the end of the fishing line, thereby asserting his view of the superiority of action over thought and at the same time fulfilling an all too evident death-wish. The others are mesmerized by his action, just as they are horrified and alienated by it. Charles survives, but Julie leaves him, appalled at his simplicity and innocence and hating the guilt she feels for having cooperated in his watery ordeal. John, the fiancé, succeeds Charles, completing a second triangle with Julie and Gilbert. He is not as ingenuous as Charles, and his understanding provides the play with an authoritiative and stable viewpoint. Nevertheless, he is as hooked as Charles and Gilbert are.

The play concludes in Venice where the brilliance of the surroundings partially offsets Julie's sense of moral humiliation: "One is encompassed by things so rich and rare / They can't be hurt by the conscience one brings to them" (122).[2] Hanging over the ending is John's question as to how they are all to survive given the burden of knowledge which they all share. John is a believer in adaptability and resilience, and says at one point: "Fluidity is proof against major disasters. / The marbles melt and wink at me. 'Survive,' / They whisper" (91). He feels that behavior requires a delicacy between people which allows for tacit ambiguities in feeling whereas the other characters appear to be grotesques, frozen into postures and attitudes that preclude movement, change and—ultimately—love.

Marine symbolism surrounds all of the characters. Julie's voracious appetite for consciousness, for example, is depicted in terms of the sea:

> I want to dive down,
> Discover, bring back whatever it is, the black
> Pearl, the sense of whatever I am,
> But my bones are full of air, my words are larks,
> The sun is sparkling on the surface of the water
> In all directions except from underneath. (98)

Julie's frustration at not being able to release the contents of her subconscious from their blue depths is an ironic parallel to Charles's vain attempt to be rational about the subconscious energies that compel him to act as he does.

The ocean symbolizes the primitive needs of the characters, including the atavistic longing for violence that lurks beneath the glossy surface of their lives. Even Charles, who otherwise seems impenetrable, learns from his agonizing immersion in the sea of unconsciousness: "Dolphin, medusa, hammerhead shark, starfish / Shall look at me henceforth with Julie's eyes" (109). His awakened consciousness of his wife's true nature does not, of course, free him from her; in fact it might be said to doom him: "Draw me from water, leave me to the fish— / You cannot save my life. I have seen your eyes" (109).

The bait motif is the most pervasive and potent symbol in the play. In a sense each of the characters is caught by the other. Gilbert, for example, uses his sister as a bait to catch Charles in order to satisfy his own unexpressed desires. Similarly, in marrying Charles Julie might be said to use him as bait to retain the love of her brother. Metaphorically, each of the characters is a fisherman, each is bait, and each has been caught and wounded. They are trapped by attractions which they cannot control, and becoming conscious of their entrapment simply increases their paralysis and pain. This is the reason for the underlying mood of stasis that seeps through the play.

The shuttling back and forth between the Gulf Stream and Venice, using the two sides of the stage, was Merrill's way of trying to prevent the prevailing stasis from suffocating the play. Venice symbolizes a world of highly developed amoral consciousness, a place of exquisite form. The Gulf Stream, on the other hand, symbolizes an arena in which moral testing takes place. The movement from one setting to another provides the play with some much needed surface action that to some extent offsets the potential monotony implicit in the characters' reveries.

Apart from the play's obvious poetic qualities—its use of soliloquies, blank verse, occasional rhyme, and symbolism—the overall structure incorporates elements that Merrill thought of as operatic—"lyrical interludes, recitatives, duets, even something I thought of as a trio."[3] The initial, surcharged mood of the play is also rather poetic—Merrill thought of it as Jacobean. At the very outset of the play the characters are tense and embroiled, which strains the audience's nerves by generating emotion before the underlying situation has been explained.

The play is kept at an elevated level both through the imagery and the dignified, measured flow of the lines. Julie's impression of the Gulf Stream is an example:

> See how the light moves through the water
> Like strings of a piano. And the water
> Is not blue but purple. Look out there!
> Think of them threading down, the strings of light,
> To where an absolute darkness begins,
> How they must sound against a thousand cutting fins. (94–95)

The poetry, here as elsewhere, is keyed to what action there is in the play. The paucity of action is the principal deficiency, though, in *The Bait*. In other respects, it offers much that is evocative and graceful.

The Immortal Husband

The Immortal Husband, a three-act play, was produced in New York
by the Artists' Theatre February 14, 1955. Merrill told Ashley Brown
that he wrote the play for the actress Anne Meacham and that the
production was *"fairly* successful."[4] The play was based on the Greek
myth of Tithonus and Aurora. When Aurora, goddess of the dawn, fell
in love with Tithonus, he asked her for the gift of eternal life. This was
granted, but as he had forgotten to ask for eternal youth, he grew older
and older while Aurora remained young and beautiful. They had one
child, a son, Memnon. At last Aurora tired of Tithonus, and just before
taking another lover turned him into a cicada, or grasshopper—or, in
the version Merrill follows, wrapped him in a cocoon.
    Merrill's intention was to provide a contemporary tone and setting
for the ancient story—like Cocteau, who seemed to Merrill to have
"melted the marble" of the Greek myths.[5] The novelty of his approach
was in furnishing each of the three acts with a different historical setting
illustrating different points in Tithonus's life as well as mirroring three
distinct social periods. Although each act begins with a new setting and
time frame, however, the same protagonists and the same types of
supporting characters appear throughout the play. To provide further
continuity, Merrill wanted only six actors to play all of the roles. He
hoped by doubling and tripling the roles to dramatize the historical
recurrence of the same kinds of archetypal figures from period to period
in spite of inevitable differences in appearance. The pattern ultimately
reinforces the play's underlying assumption that ancient Greek myths
are relevant to contemporary experience. Merrill filled in his design by
employing in each of the three acts dialogue in the dramatic style of a
particular period. The first act, set in Victorian England, employs a
genteel style. The second act is patterned after Chehkov, while the
third, set in contemporary America, has a colloquial style fitting the
period.
    Act I opens in 1854 in England when Tithonus is twenty. He is ill at
ease under the authority of Laomedon, a rigid, Victorian father who
reeks of decorum. Laomedon lectures his son on the need to do
something with his life, a need that escapes Tithonus in the first,
euphoric phase of his immortality. The conflict between Laomedon and

Tithonus, while conventional enough in some respects, touches on the
theme of the value of time which is central to the play. The first act
opens up the dramatic possibilities symbolized by the union of
Tithonus and Aurora. What will life be like for a human being who is
given immortality? What will happen to a goddess who acquires
human emotions?

In a symbolic sense Laomedon and Aurora can be seen as aspects of
Tithonus's interior struggle to decide what to do with his life. Laomedon points in the direction of responsibility and morality while Aurora
calls him to pleasure, love, personal knowledge, and beauty. Although
Tithonus chooses Aurora's way, he does so partly out of inexperience
with life and partly out of a fear of death and mutability: "Change is
what I've always hated—to see people, like leaves on fire, twisted and
crumpled by life." He rejects Mrs. Mallow's useful commonplace that
dying is "part of life" (173).[6] Aurora is no help to him since she, even
more than he, misunderstands the value of mortality. Act I ends as
symmetrically as it began. As the marriage of Tithonus and Aurora had
offset the death of Tithonus's mother, the discovery of the bleak
immortality that awaits Tithonus undermines the bliss which the
lovers feel. At the close Aurora experiences human emotion by shed-
ding her first tears without understanding why, while Tithonus goes off
to brood with an all too vivd understanding of his situation.

Act II opens in Russia in 1894 when Tithonus is nearly 60. An
autumnal setting has replaced the late spring of the first act. As in Act I
Tithonus and Aurora are flanked by finite lovers (Konstantin and
Fanya) who act as foils to their immortal union. Tithonus has matured
into a disillusioned dilettante while Aurora, though as young and
beautiful as ever, appears to have acquired a very human taste for irony.
In an effort to revive their relationship, she has become pregnant.
However, the dialogue between Tithonus and Olga, an old, dying
woman provides the dramatic focus in Act II. In a typical exchange
Tithonus comments on how agreeable life would be if only its beautiful
moments "would not pass away." To which Olga replies: "Agreeable
things *do* pass away. That is how we distinguish them from disagreeable
things" (206). She leads Tithonus gradually to an understanding of
what, in his partial escape from time, he has lost. Above all, she teaches
him about the fruitfulness of change. In one scene Tithonus tells her of
his approval of young Konstantin's intransigent opposition to compromise, and she responds: "Never to compromise? But you pass up a
great blessing! Compromise is to our souls what sleep is to our bodies.

And who would choose never to sleep? It is the compromise of the body with death, a delicious thing! We don't agree" (201).

The contrast between Tithonus and Olga encompasses not only what they say but their different stakes in saying it. Tithonus is pedagogical and remote in dealing with the issues of change, time, and death while Olga feels she must urgently resolve these matters for herself in the little time she has remaining. Reflecting Merrill's fondness for dualism, the two challenge each other in order to sift the strength and ultimately the reality of their own positions. Ironically, Tithonus, the opponent of change, is himself altered by the encounter conceding at last that he has "not had a happy life" (204). Olga's belief in reincarnation, which incorporates aspects of both death and renewal, silhouettes the sterile continuum of Tithonus's longevity. Ironically, the only experience of renewal Tithonus has in the play is his contact with a dying woman with whom he comes to feel an "extraordinary ease, as though something clogged had been set running again, a stopped watch shaken and set running" (203).

In Act III, which is set in America in the 1950s, Tithonus is 120 years of age, withered in mind and body and centered completely and querulously upon himself. Aurora, now gripped by revulsion at the sight of him, leaves him to go off with Mark, consigning Tithonus to a nurse. Aurora's rising vitality parallels Tithonus's degeneration, including an obvious loss of intellectual power. Aurora, moreover, retains the capacity to be stimulated by new experience. She declares herself "weary of obligations" (218), and, having reverted to a life centered in the pleasure of the present moment once again, announces that she has "no destiny" (234).

Structurally, the play comes full circle when Mark has the opportunity, which Tithonus had had, of joining Aurora in an immortal pact. He declines telling Aurora: "Just let me keep my own mortality, which you will have made precious" (234). His ironic reply, which he expects her not to understand, sums up the play's principal theme: in a brush with the immortal the hidden value of human nature, rather than being overshadowed as one might think, is unexpectedly illuminated. Some of the characters feel the play's theme instinctively—as does the gardener in Act I, who on hearing that Tithonus had been made immortal, quips: "I don't know as how I'd enjoy *that*!" (189)

Tithonus's immunity from death initially makes him insensitive not only to his own death but to the suffering and death of others, thus depriving himself of his moral and emotional connection with the rest of humanity. This can be seen in his sudden loss of interest in the plight of the tree that is slowly being killed by mistletoe in Act I as well as in his increasingly narcissistic turn of mind, which is symbolized in the ring he wears:

> TITHONUS: The ring I wear comes from the Bazaar in Constan-
> tinople. A serpent, you see, with its tail in its
> mouth.
> FANYA: It makes me shiver.
> TITHONUS: It is a symbol of eternity and of wisdom.
> OLGA: Also of evil, I've been told. (200)

The triptych structure of *The Immortal Husband* permitted Merrill to anchor his mythic story in the concreteness of history. The social settings provided for each of the three acts add density to the play's themes through the introduction of historical overtones. The stern God of the Victorians, for example, is satirized in Aurora's portrait of Zeus in the first act: "He's fearfully bad-tempered, or can be. It's quite prover-bial. . . . There's a whole etiquette involved. You have to sort of crouch beside him, with your left hand on his knees and your right hand fiddling with his beard" (186). This picture of Victorian divinity weights the play's emotion in favor of the mortal characters. Similarly, in Act II Konstantin's whimsical resolve to, as his "first reform," herd chaperones out in their black dresses to be "shot like turkeys" foreshadows the spilling of blood in an actual Russian Revolution (193). The scene with its shadowy portent obliquely points up Tithonus's aloof withdrawal from history—either the Czarist twilight in Russia or in the other periods and cultures used in the play.

The most important visual motif in the play is the contrast of light and darkness. As the goddess of the dawn Aurora is characteristically associated with the rising sun, being pictured on one occasion as wearing a "Chinese robe of the clearest blue" (207), while on another occasion she alludes to herself as the "rosy-fingered one" (183). Merrill employs the imagery of light in connection with Aurora in such a way that its limitations as well as its luster are revealed. Even Tithonus eventually perceives that true vision consists in seeing "in the dark, the way a cat does." Understanding, he tells Aurora, has ultimately to do with "suffering" and "tears" rather than with light (184). Similarly, Enid says in Act III: "I love to look over the side of a boat. You can see your face in the water if it's calm and you're turned away from the sun. Not a reflection really, a kind of dark transparency" (220). Conversely, in Act I Tithonus laments the flood of light that accompanies his immortality: "I have remembered everything and experienced nothing. Sunlight in cities, brilliance of theaters, the phosphorescence of names and places in the mind bent on darkness—nothing but light, light, light! It is not to be borne" (208).

A secondary line of imagery in the play has to do with plants. Sometimes these images (e.g., the apple tree in Act I) assume allegorical significance. Plant imagery is also connected with the play's theme of growth. In the exchange between Tithonus and Olga in Act II her suggestion that they have met in a previous life prompts Tithonus to remark: "What you said just now—reverberates. There is a stirring, as of roots at the end of winter" (204). Later Olga observes that with the coming of age one can "uproot" one's wants "as I have done. Where I had planted an alley of chrysanthemums there is now a little row of herbs" (206). Plants are also used as a touchstone of the characters' attitudes. At the opening of Act II, for instance, Aurora's irritation at her garden reflects her bitterness, exhaustion, and disappointment in the human condition.

In spite of the play's weighty themes Merrill keeps the texture light and the tone relaxed and informal. Even the most troubled moments are shot through with comedy. There is the lugubrious decline of Tithonus in the last act, for example, as well as the hilarious character names (e.g., "Emily Mandible," "Claude Delice") which lift the play in its gloomiest phase. *The Immortal Husband* exhibits a fine mingling of thought and action as well as an impressive skill in structuring. Merrill avoided the dreamlike sententiousness that at times weakens *The Bait* by rounding his characters and by making more immediate and plausible the exchanges between them than those depicted in the earlier play. If it had not been for his increasing impatience with the enormous amount of time expended in dramatic production, he might have developed into a formidable presence in the American theater. As it was, after 1955 he decided to pursue his interest in the drama within the boundaries of his novels and poems.

Chapter Three
Fiction

Short Stories

Merrill once confided that he enjoyed reading fiction "more often—or more profoundly" than he enjoyed reading poems, adding that there was no poet "except perhaps Dante whose work has the extraordinary richness of Tolstoy or Proust."[1] In addition to his two novels Merrill has published two short stories, "Driver" and "Peru: The Landscape Game." "Driver" (1962) centers on a middle-aged man named Walker who becomes obsessed with driving. Beginning in 1919, he drives his way through life as a traveling salesman up until the 1960s. In one sense Walker is a parody of the nomadic American folk hero, driven by a need to escape the settled condition and always on the lookout for fresh encounters with the Absolute. On another level he is caught up, as was Tithonus in "The Immortal Husband," in a ludicrous misuse of time. Rather than driving headlong through time in an effort to escape it, he should—the tale makes abundantly clear—learn to "walk," as his name suggests (505).[2]

The automobile in Walker's hands becomes an extension of himself as well as his final reference and refuge. For example, he develops erotic feelings about his automobile, which at the same time becomes a menace to everyone else. The tale wryly explores the relationship between the organic and the mechanical. An old rustic couple whom Walker picks up symbolize the natural world: "They were brown and wrinkled, dressed in patched blacks and raveling grays. The woman wore knitted stockings. In both hands she held a coffee can planted with herbs." Her husband carries a basket of apples, "pocked, misshapen ones which nevertheless had been beautifully polished" (494). They give Walker an apple, which he throws away as too "bitter" and "hard" (495). The apple is time, drudgery, suffering, and possibly love, mortal circumstances that Walker seeks to escape.

Nevertheless, the encounter with the farm family breaks down some of his isolation, and he determines to be more open in future. He marries one of his passengers, a "poor, foolish, virgin librarian" from Iowa named Muriel (498). Ironically, she also is trying to escape life's dreariness. Unlike Walker, however, she is capable of love. After Walker's inevitable separation from Muriel he enters a hallucinatory episode in which he drives two psychics to a deserted, rural airfield where their messianic journey to the universe is expected to begin. Seeing how forlorn they are and perhaps reflecting on his own wasted life, he becomes suddenly possessed by a vision of the airplane as a pleasure dome par excellence: "Driving, I kept glancing skyward, prepared, in spite of everything, for the glint of wings. Cross with myself, miles from my road, how gladly I would have hailed an order of machine superior to mine. To this day I cannot see a plane without stopping to wonder, to reenter those last lonely hours in the car—the mirror, face up beside me, shooting provocative flashes into the bare heavens" (506).

The story's pronounced sexual language is set in ironic juxtaposition with its religious imagery. Toward the end, for example, Walker recalls the "missions" of his youth and the "awakenings" he had dreamed of bringing to his fellow man (503). Earlier, he had described the cars of the 1920s as imperfectly manufactured "Pilgrims out of faith, theirs and mine" (492). Similarly, when he decides to pick up riders, he thinks of himself as inspired by the "missionary's fervor" to acquaint others with the "Revelation" of the automobile (495–96). The interlacing of sexual and religious motifs links Walker's otherwise bizarre life with central human experiences. Thus, while on an individual level he is an allegorical figure, a sort of personified libido, on another level he mirrors his society's infatuation with the machine. The story's wit arises from its rational tone and amoral vantage point. Walker's life is told from his own dispassionate point of view, allowing the reader to savor dramatic irony after dramatic irony while awakening soberly to the uncomfortable social relevance of his experience.

Both "Driver" and "Peru: The Landscape Game" focus on the mind of a single character who tells his own story. If Walker is in the dark throughout his story, however, it is the reader who finds himself groping in "Landscape Game." Here the reader encounters a sophisticated and imaginative observer who appears to be well ahead of his own story. "Peru: The Landscape Game" is J's account of his journey to Lima, Cuzco, and the Inca ruins at Machu Picchu. The motifs of travel and landscape are made ambiguous at the outset, though, when J describes a psychological game he and his companion, K, have been introduced to by an old Swiss lady at the Hotel Périchole in Lima. The game involves an imaginary walk away from a house in which each player discovers on the way "a key, a bowl, a body of water, a wild creature, and finally a wall." The house, the woman explains, is "your own life, your notion of it. Trees round about stand for Other People. The key is Religion. The bowl, Art. The water, Sex. The wild thing is Yourself—the unconscious. The wall is Death."[3] Small wonder that K thinks the Swiss lady is Jung's widow.

The story reaches its climax when J and K play the landscape game using the house and character of their guide, Porfirio, as their point of departure. Their differing views of Porfirio give rise to the feeling that they may not be suitable traveling companions after all. K, for example, perceives Porfirio's character as a "key" to the mystery of the Incas while J's view is more protective and realistic; he sees Porfirio as having been exploited and diminished by history and tourism and thus unlikely to yield much in the way of esoteric knowledge. Earlier in the story the game had already illuminated the deepest cleavage in the natures of the two travelers. K's fantasies of a ferocious polar bear and his vision of a "high brick wall complete with electrified alarm system, enclosing the estate of an industrial magnate" reveal a repressed, volatile personality that contrasts with J's serener landscape—"a pond stagnant in appearance but full of activity: lily pads, tadpoles, buzzing dragonflies" (106). J's 'wall' illustrates his relaxed acceptance of the natural interfusion of life and death, a "stone wall exactly my height, over which appear eaves and chimneys of a house much like the one I started out from" (106).

Toward the end Merrill lets fly his narrative thunderbolt. The trip to Peru has been an imagined one, a landscape game prior to any enacted in the story. The purpose of the game is for J to test the value of a contemplated journey by running it through his mind first. Having done so, he decides to set out alone without the company of K. The Jungian motif of the landscape game adds an anthropological dimension to the story in a study of group versus individual consciousness. A maid in the hotel, for example, is thought not to have a "soul" in the sense of an "individual resonance to this or that. But she knows how to live 12,000 feet above the sea," J hastily adds (108). Both J and K perceive the Incas and their straggling descendants as intensely communal. Thought for them is assumed to be part of the common breath, and is generated without individual effort from every corner of their surroundings.

Paradoxically, however, the archetypal symbols that leap from the imaginations of J and K during their playing of the landscape game reflect a history that is no less atavistic. The result is that the question of individuality hangs over the story at its close. Nonetheless, it is implied that man's essential power as a creature lies in his imagination, whether in the form of the towering architecture of the Incas or in the intricate and ingenious game which J and K play and which in a sense Merrill plays with the reader. The story exhibits a superb handling of ambiguity and suspense and is rich in intellectual challenge and buried significance, a design highly typical of Merrill's narrative art.

The Seraglio

Merrill's first novel, *The Seraglio* (1957), which is partly autobiographical in its general outline, centers on the life of Francis Tanning, the introspective son of a Long Island financier, Benjamin Tanning. Francis, twenty-five, returns from a sojourn in Italy to be with his ailing father and to offer support to his mother, who has become isolated after her divorce from Tanning. At the beginning of the novel Benjamin has lost interest in his third wife and is looking around, in spite of his maladies, for a replacement. Francis's dilemma is that he is so overpowered by his father that he is unable to develop his own male identity. He introduces into the house an attractive though no longer young European sculptress in an attempt to have someone mediate between himself and his father, but it doesn't work. Finally, in terror and confusion over his sexual identity he attempts suicide through castration, and thus ironically prepares himself for the role of eunuch in his father's seraglio, a position which he takes up with surprising equanimity at the end of the novel.

Most of the action takes place at Benjamin Tanning's huge "cottage" on Long Island, but there are important scenes as well in Jamaica and

Rome. Francis's point of view dominates the first half of *The Seraglio,*
while there is a range of viewpoints in the second half, including those
of Irene Cheek, who hopes to become the fourth Mrs. Tanning, the
sculptress Xenia Grosz, Francis's student friend, Jane, and Lady Prudence Good, the resourceful English woman who does become the
fourth Mrs. Tanning. Merrill's switching of the pattern of point of view
permits the reader to see Francis as others see him, just as the reader
comes to know these people through Francis's viewpoint in the first part
of the novel. Merrill's handling of point of view in *The Seraglio* shows an
impressive grasp of narrative economy.

He portrays Francis as struggling to find his own view of reality
amidst other realities that surround him and that had shaped him. In
this respect the relationship between Francis and his father is characterized by pressure, pain, and by occasional accommodation and good
feeling. The complexity of the relationship can be seen in Francis's
implicit sense that his father has emasculated him psychologically and
yet deeply desires his son to produce the offspring which will confirm
his own virile hold on the future. Thus, while Benjamin continually
undermines his already insecure son, he also tries to school him in the
stalking of women. The path taken by Benjamin Tanning cannot be
taken by his son, and yet the father points to no other: such is the
impasse that forms the dramatic center of *The Seraglio.* Francis waits
miserably and in vain for some "word of reassurance" from his father,
some "sign from the one who had lived so much, to show that life was
no prerogative of his own—that it might equally be the road he,
Francis, traveled" (57).[4]

From his father Francis derives his terrifying view of sexuality as
"violent," a matter of "anguish, lies, recriminations" (55). Thus, when
Benjamin jokingly tells Francis early in the novel that he leaves the
seraglio in his hands, the young man understands ruefully that his role
will be that of "keeper" rather than hereditary sultan (65–66). On the
other hand, Benjamin's illness, which reduces him to the figure of a
wounded lion, appears to create the opportunity for sympathy between
father and son. Some of the old man's words to his son are tinged with
pathos and tenderness, if also with delusion: "Don't you think it's
strange that you and I should be so lonely?" he asks Francis on one
occasion: "I've been lonely all my life, and I think you will be" (58).

The divorce of Francis's parents left him in his mother's care for much of his childhood and adolescence, and the male identity he absorbed was largely her soft and genteel image of manhood. His mother's primness, which complements his father's lustiness and histrionics, leaves Francis admiring "women who didn't weep and men who openly, like his father, did" (88). More fundamentally, however, if his father intimidates Francis, his mother saps his desire to enter into life at all: "Squaring her shoulders, opening her book, she had affected him as living on where life itself had ceased—or been so lived, so used, that nothing was left but the past and the vantage from which she saw it, perfect, remote, hers" (36).

The effect of both parents is to prolong Francis's sojourn in childhood. While physically and intellectually an adult, he lingers emotionally in childhood, confiding to his friend Jane at one point that he was "tired of grown-ups" (90). Francis's desire to prolong childhood is shown in his unsuccessful attempt to renounce his wealth. The terms in which he does so make it evident that he rejects the corruptive and imprisoning effect of wealth but also that he fears the power that wealth brings. In addition, he avoids sexual intimacy with women, which would compel him to compete with the kind of adulthood symbolized by his father. The homosexuality that surfaces in the middle of the novel thus offers Francis a way out.

Part Two of the novel reveals Francis's newfound independence while at the same time subordinating his point of view to those of others in order to dramatize the folding of his own existence into the broad stream of life. Aware of how bizarre his new life looks to others, he nonetheless wins their respect, if not their confidence. The psychic energy that allows him to declare and openly follow his own tastes is amplified by the setting and imagery, which altogether suggest his reincarnation as a Faustian figure who, not without cost, has taken charge of his own fate. Appropriately, demonic strains are heard throughout the novel's second section.

A particularly successful aspect of *The Seraglio*'s structure is the use of a subplot involving Francis's sister, Enid, and her daughter, Lily, to amplify the parent/child motif that pervades the novel. In order to draw attention to Enid and Lily's story, Merrill opens *The Seraglio* with the incident involving Lily's slashing of the portrait of Enid that hung in the Tanning house. The slashing, which resulted from Lily's resentment at being ignored by her mother, serves as a touchstone to illuminate the major characters. With characteristic egocentricity, for instance, Benjamin Tanning assumes that the act was directed against himself.

The act was in fact a child's testing of parental power:

With the tip of the silver knife she caressed, as with a wand, her mother's features, traced the curve of the lips, the eyebrows and cheek. The faint grating gave her gooseflesh. Resting the point against the surface at a certain angle, she saw how the blade reflected the whole face dully, in miniature distortion. She moved it this way and that; her mother vanished, reappeared. Before long a puzzlement came over her, to see that a speck of paint, no bigger than a gnat's wing, had chipped away, leaving a tiny patch of paler color beneath. How? When? Just at the corner of her mother's eye, in which a streak of white created an uncanny liveliness. Lily's heart began to pound. She wouldn't have dreamed this face could be so fragile. (7–8)

Lily's discovery of her mother's vulnerability foreshadows the main-plot relationship between Francis and his father. Children in the world of *The Seraglio* hunger for affection from their parents and receive instead a lesson in how to manipulate the lives of others. Amid such surroundings children like Lily learn to be reserved and covert. The lesson of decorum is symbolized in the novel in the restoration of the painting, which is so expertly done that Francis finds it difficult to tell where it had been torn. Francis plays the role of intermediary between the apparently impossible extremes of parent and child both for himself and—through his relationship with Lily—on behalf of children in general. The need for such a role is satirically and devastatingly depicted in the culminating image of the christening cake. On top of the cake are decorative candy infants which the adults devour with relish. The cannibalistic relationship between parent and child, which is symbolized by the cake, is so close to reality that Francis remarks, not altogether humorously, that the children should have been given a cake "with parents on it" (310).

The power of Merrill's portrayal of parents and children stems from his ability to demonstrate the one-sidedness of the relationship in subtle and unremarkable but telling detail. Francis's meeting with his mother, for example, which follows the year in Europe that was to have been his emancipation, induces the following response in him: "Glancing back from her bedroom door, he saw that she had already put on her glasses and reopened her book, squaring her shoulders as she began to read. It was a gesture he had forgotten, and it touched him as much as any she had made all afternoon" (34–35). The largeness of parent in relation to child stamps the child's memory with an impression that is indelibly and melodramatically vivid. Larry Buchanan, for example, appears larger than life to his daughter, Lily: "She watched him drink. His high coloring and the brilliant shades he liked in his shirts and ties—broad stripes of orange and olive against pink, or deep yellow checkered with black, brick reds, purples, apple greens—overpowered the pale settings contrived for them. How fiercely, for example, his cigar glowed now!" (11). The mythic proportions of the parental image lodged within the child's psyche stand out with exaggerated intensity in the case of Benjamin Tanning. To Francis he is still a "Moses who, white-haired and wise, had nonetheless never shaken off some early magic, half memory, half myth, of women glimmering down upon the gently rocking raft of reeds" (80).

Much of the symbolism in the novel ties in with the theme of childhood. An example is the gold ring which Francis had purchased in an antique shop in Rome and which had come from the grave of a dead child of the fourth century. The ring comes to symbolize the state of childhood, its softness especially suggesting the vulnerable malleability of that state. Significantly, Francis gives the ring to Lily as a sign of his own departure from childhood and as a sympathetic token of his understanding of her plight. He gives it to her as an invitation to participate in life, as he himself is finally resolved to do. It "must be *worn*," he tells her when she worries about the ring's softness: "Things must be used. If they break, it can't be helped" (214).

Another important line of imagery in the novel is that of draining. The book's most memorable scenes are those in which Benjamin Tanning thrashes about in a vain effort to hold back the vanishing waters of his manhood, furious at being "*drained* by people he cared nothing about" (126). The maid, Alice, cautions Lily early in the book to keep in mind that childhood "ought to be the happiest part" of her life and that Lily's was "draining away like a lovely warm bath while she scrambled to replace the plug" (13). A counter image to the draining motif is that of the pearl, a ubiquitous symbol in Merrill's writings for the beneficent working of time. The two motifs are brought into sharp juxtaposition in a symbolic view of the Buchanan home: "The large

room was done in tones of cream and sugar. On bright days, with only
the dotted-swiss curtains drawn, it seemed the inside of a pearl. Lily's
advance through its present gloom could not be heard above her father's
distant thrashing in his tub" (13).

The boundary between reality and unreality is tested repeatedly in
The Seraglio, usually inconclusively. Seeing her mutilated son in the
hospital, for example, Vinnie reflects that the experience was as "real as
a nightmare" (175). In another scene Francis has a dream, lying next to
Xenia, in which he becomes his father, a role which he subconsciously
and gratefully accepts in the dream even if it is one that he both rejects
and feels inadequate to fill in his waking life. The most elaborate dream
in *The Seraglio* is that provided by the composer, Thomas Utter, who
has written an opera based on the myth of Orpheus. The opera amplifies
the Faustian aura that already surrounds Francis in the middle section of
the book as well as serving as a lurid mirror of most of the cast of *The
Seraglio:*

Before them, beyond the glowing apron of the stage, could be distinguished
the lights and boxes of a theater so like their own that a vast mirror might
have been set up inside the proscenium. The view being from the vantage of
the stage itself, hence unfamiliar to most, heightened the illusion. Gilt and
puce, cherub and luster, all had been copied. Somewhere infernal musicians
tuned their instruments. The ranks of the damned chattered, called to one
another, ruffled their libretti or wielded great plumed fans, wiped steam
from monocles—there was a sense of extreme heat—until at a nod from a
horned demon in white tie, a bit elevated above the unseen players, the
music began. (261)

If on one level the opera mirrors the perverse machinations of the
Tanning and Buchanan households, it also symbolizes Francis's somewhat guilty revolt against a conventional lifestyle.

In the third and final section of the book Francis finds himself in
unexpected equilibrium with the external world. He finds, for example, that the Dundees, who had struck him as such preposterous
American provincials in Italy, look pleasing and natural against their
native background. Bertha Dundee now looks "perfectly nice, delight-
ful really. Seeing her where she belonged, against a whitening sky and
flat sea, Francis found in her exactly the kind of cool artificial prettiness
he most liked" (304). Though touched with irony, the passage reveals
his underlying acceptance of himself.

One of the strengths of *The Seraglio* is its exquisite attention to setting. The description of the rococo styling of Francis's apartment in Part Two is particularly memorable. More impressive even than this is the way in which Merrill portrays the shaping power of setting in relationship to his characters' lives. The impact of setting on action is quietly dramatized early in the novel in a scene in which Francis ponders the awesome effect of the ocean room in his father's house: ". . . how the room sustained Enid! how it sustained, against his will, himself! Even a *real* child entering there would have had to sit as Francis did, its little legs crossed, talking of the weather, refusing a second chocolate, charmed into forgetting the friends outside who waited to play leap-frog or "games" in a garage attic. Wouldn't it help, he brooded, to leap up, cry out, smash something? But the room met his eye so trustingly; it was easier to do violence to himself" (64).

The Tanning estate is the centerpiece of the novel, each of its details generating a sense of the drama within. The guest house area where Francis is put up, for example, is a tableau of the novel's intrigues, a set of four, small buildings that "faced one another like card-players, over a square of gravel" (40). The main house, whose steep roof resembles those of houses in "fairy-tales" (6), in other respects symbolizes the meretriciousness of the American dream, both the house and its inhabitants reminding one strongly of *The Great Gatsby*. The other major settings are Italy and Jamaica. To Francis Italy represents both formal beauty and an alternative to the affluent unreality of America: "He had wanted the cold tile floors and the smelly stove. The bareness appealed to him, like that of the straight razor he affected; it made *him* seem more real" (20). Merrill uses the Jamaican setting to suggest the mass of humanity beyond the Tanning household. Jamaica is where the rich gather among the poor, as Irene Cheek realizes when she looks out at the "rows of black figures watching from behind the barbed wire where her property ended." Self-consciously, she becomes aware of herself as one of "two or three dozen white women watched by those hundreds that wholly blotted out the sea's shining" (182–83). In like vein, the death of Sir Edward Good, who had exploited hundreds of black workers at his molasses factory, is given moral significance when his car is fatally diverted from the road by the sudden appearance of a "a cart jammed with Negroes" (218).

In spite of the brunt of such scenes Merrill modulates the tone and mood of *The Seraglio* in order to steer a course between gravity and levity. Most of the characters are portrayed mock-heroically at some point, sometimes simply by being given names like Lady Prudence Good and Irene Cheek. In addition, Merrill's fine ear for dialogue, which vividly captures the conniving of Irene Cheek and the fuming of Benjamin Tanning, adds liveliness to a novel that is otherwise somewhat lacking in action. The dialogue is studded with aphorisms, and—as in *The Immortal Husband*—the aphorisms have a way of wandering into unsuspected depths. For example, on learning that there is a new medication that would leave his father's heart free of pain, Francis wonders aloud to Enid about the wisdom of such a drug: "I mean, doesn't pain serve to warn him when he goes too far, physically or otherwise?" Enid answers with epigrammatic acuteness that pain "teaches us what we *can't* avoid"—to which her brother mutely assents (63). *The Seraglio* is especially memorable, though, because of its visual richness and refined analysis of motive and feeling. Merrill's cameo portrait of the expatriates, Francis and Jane, against the light of Rome early in the novel will serve as a final, concise example of *The Seraglio*'s descriptive power: "They were sitting after all like cut flowers, up to their calves in the purest water" (18). Few contemporary novels, it can be affirmed, have offered as much to the eye.

The (Diblos) Notebook

In spite of Merrill's doubts about his future as a novelist, his second novel, *The (Diblos) Notebook* (1965), was nominated for the National Book Award. He had originally entitled the book "The Poros Notebook," after the Greek island on which the novel is set. He changed the name to *Diblos* after the Greek word *dibolos,* which means "two-pointed," an allusion to the theme of dualism that is at the heart of the novel. He placed the name *Diblos* in parentheses in order to suggest the tentative nature of the book's title and contents. In his notes for the novel Merrill described his technique as "revelatory."[5] As in the case of certain paintings, the novel was to reveal its treasures through its *pentimenti,* breaks in the finished surface that revealed earlier stages in the creative process, the "small rips and ripples," as Merrill put it, "that make us know there *is* a fabric of illusion."[6]

Merrill offers tissue sections of a novel in various stages of growth so that the reader is able to compare the freshness and erratic qualities of an early draft with the polish and cohesiveness of a revised version. The alternation of novelist's diary and inset novel is carefully weighted so that, although the sequence appears spontaneous and random, the narrator's life and circumstances occupy most of the first half of the notebook while the inset novel dominates the second half. In unpublished notes Merrill declared that he wanted the reader to glimpse much more than the modest plot that underlies the novel. He had become attracted to the idea of writing a notebook belonging to a character who was trying to write what he himself had been trying to write. Furthermore, the notebook format would demand that there be included the "usual welter of irrelevance: laundry lists, addresses, self-conscious 'thinking' about Life and Art, tiny notations of detail which would never have been incorporated into any of the roughly written and re-written scenes."[7]

While the technique inevitably led to fragmentariness, it also prevented staleness by eliminating the need to develop and to round things off. Merrill foresaw the most profound effect of his technique as being the interplay between the notebook writer's life and the lives of his characters, the "endless parrying of the fictive characters with certain prototypes in the notebook-keeper's 'real' experience" which would make the reader at least as curious about the notebook writer's life as about the lives of his characters.[8] Gradually, the reader would realize that the narrator's half-expressed drama was the real center of the book.

The plot of *The (Diblos) Notebook* involves four characters: two real brothers, the narrator and Orson, and two fictive brothers, Sandy and Orestes, who are based on the real ones. Apart from the interplay between the fictive and the real, which is the narrative core of *Diblos,* Merrill's notes reveal that he thought of himself as working toward a definitive, novelistic portrayal of brotherhood: "The word 'grandmother' thanks to Proust will have wind in its sails for the rest of time. Why should I shrink from doing my best for 'brother,' or 'half my best for half-brother?' "[9]

The notebook is the narrator's record of a series of happenings on the island of Diblos as well as of his attempts to write a novel about those happenings. The central character in his projected novel is Orestes, who is based on the narrator's older half-brother, Orson, a Greek-American who seven years earlier had come to Greece on a sabbatical leave. As Orson had done, Orestes becomes involved with Dora, the widow of a

Greek painter. Orestes takes Dora with him to the United States at the
end of his leave only to discover that she fits incongruously into her
American surroundings. Their relationship dissolves, but through
their marriage of convenience, Dora manages to stay on in America,
opting for American culture as Orestes's mother had also done. The
Notebook reaches its denouement with the return to Diblos of the real
brother, Orson. Attempting to take possession of some things he had
left in the cottage Dora had lent him, he is met by her son, Byron, who,
infuriated at Orson's treatment of his mother, gives him a whipping.
The *Notebook* concludes with a reunion of the narrator and Orson and
with the narrator's resolve to give up the novel in its incomplete state.

Part of the inset novel is given over to the differing boyhoods of
Sandy and Orestes. Orestes had been raised in poverty in the immigrant
tenements of New York whereas Sandy had been raised comfortably in
his American father's house in Houston. The mother, Eleni, is depicted
as more adaptable than either of her sons, having learned how to survive
in two very different marriages and two markedly distinct cultures. The
jealousy of the half-brothers for the love of the mother they share is one
of the potent, submerged forces in the projected novel. Orestes, in
particular, sensing himself as belonging to his mother's rejected Greek
past, throws himself with neurotic intensity into an identification with
that past. In parallel fashion, having his own hybrid origins to consider,
the narrator ponders the question of his identity dimly aware that before
he can settle the matter he must come to terms with his brother. In a
sense the projected novel is his way of exploring his relationship to
Orson, which is one of the reasons why he gives up the novel once he
understands that relationship.

The narrator's daily impressions of Diblos and its 1800 inhabitants
anchor the *Notebook* in the factual present, thereby freeing his mind on
other occasions to probe more subjective areas. The intertwining of
foreground action and inset, novelistic event can be seen when the
narrator looks across the strip of water that separates the island of Diblos
from the mountainous mainland. Characteristically, his impressions
leave a mark on the novel he is writing: "From the postoffice (no letters
yet) a strange view of the Sleeping Woman, seen only by afternoon light
until today. Barely recognizable, a collapsing tent of whitish bluffs &
uncertain distances; let Orestes see her that way just before (after?) the
confrontation on the terrace" (5–6).[10] Similarly, the novel's progress is
often impeded by the narrator's fidgety ambivalence toward his brother,

giving the notebook an arrhythmic mood of nervous energy. Further contributing to a mood of flux are the narrator's continuous, shifting impressions, which at times threaten the evolving design of his novel: "How to keep recent impressions from intruding? I would never have written yesterday's last paragraph, so tortuous & smug, had it not been for Mrs. N.'s saying that Dora 'had a place in society.' The phrase clung & tickled; I've had to scratch it compulsively, thus breaking the skin of my story" (47).

Increasingly bewildered by the interplay of the fictive and the real, the narrator finds that he has to alter the way things actually happened (as in the case of Dora's offer of the cottage to Orson) because real life is at times too implausible. At other times, life is too flat so that he has to stage, for example, the poetic road meeting of Orestes and Dora rather than having her introduced to him by Mr. N. as occurred in fact. Such choices of the fictive over the real are consistent with the narrator's ironic impression that art frequently provides the archetypes upon which actual life is based. He feels this acutely in connection with Mr. and Mrs. N.: "I had been wondering in what previous life I'd encountered the N.'s—or where they had found themselves. It was in the pages of Proust" (25). Similarly, in looking at Dora's garden, he reflects that one recognized it "not from life but from productions of Chekhov" (35). Occasionally, the fictive and the actual reach a point of identity. The narrator cannot shake off the actual name, Dora, for his heroine, for example, because it so perfectly suits both his and Orestes's Byzantine conception of her. The entanglement of the fictive and real reaches its apex in the stunning actuality of Byron's whipping of Orson. The narrator finds himself overcome by the power of this scene, which, he reflects with chagrin, he would never have "dared to construct" (143).

The hopeless knotting of the fictive and the real, which contributes to the narrator's decision finally to abandon his novel, is part of a larger motif, that of the ineradicable dualism of all things. The motif is embedded in the setting of the novel—with the island of Diblos divided by a narrow strait from the Peloponnesian mainland so that an observer is always stereoscopically conscious of both landscapes. Moreover, the doubleness of the land setting is multiplied by the mirror of the sea. There are two sets of brothers, two cultures, two time frames, two standards of reality (fictive and actual), and so on. Changes in perspective, instead of simplifying the prevalent dualism, simply throw light on fresh pairs of antitheses. Dora, for example, who at first sight appears to symbolize Greece (since that is what Orestes wants her to symbolize) is in fact a hybrid, her parents having come from Russia to settle on Crete.

In some respects *The (Diblos) Notebook* conforms to the international novel pioneered by Henry James in which characters separated by different cultures struggle, often unsuccessfully, to come together. The survivors in Merrill's novel are those who adapt quickly to the new culture, as first Eleni and then Dora do. Merrill adds to the complexity of his international novel, however, the outline of a third culture, Greek-American, the ethnic wilderness inhabited by the narrator/ Sandy and Orson/Orestes. Greek-Americans are portrayed as combining the ugliness of both cultures without having the grace of either. Greek-American investors, for example, are depicted as defacing their Hellenic homeland by filling it with American restaurants and bars, leading to the "virtual disappearance of tavernas in Athens" (23).

In the face of the indissoluble mixture of Greek and American elements within him Orestes is pictured in the inset novel as turning toward a formal dualism of ideas with a kind of relief. His lecture in Athens is entitled: "The Tragic Dualism in Man." Orestes's tortured sense of identity reaches its nadir in New York when he tastelessly presents Dora as the Greek ambassadress and when he compels her to speak Greek on the telephone to his mother, who is no longer able to reciprocate. Ironically, the beleaguered Dora sees in Orestes's mad machinations the signs of his American identity: "She glimpsed the larger, national mystery behind his manners, that pendulum swinging from childish artlessness to artless maturity and back again" (107). The shallowness of Orestes's dualistic categories is further underscored by the view, shared by both the narrator and Dora, that manners constitute a more profound division between people, whether "royalty or peasants," than nationality (46).

In the hall of mirrors which constitutes the novel's structure Orestes's deformed reactions reflect the narrator's divided feelings toward his brother. Sandy, the narrator's alter ego in the inset novel, characteristically portrays his brother sharply and satirically. His view of Orestes, like the narrator's view of Orson, is obsessive and is flecked with fear and desire. At the same time, Sandy clings to Orestes as a touchstone of his personal reality, recognizing, for example, that his own friendship with Dora amounted to merely "some slight retrograde expertise in the wider heavens of Orestes' life" from which the two of them were to "return his light" (67). Through his surrogate, Sandy, the narrator struggles throughout the *Notebook* to free himself from his fear of Orson's love for him, a love that he finally returns at the end of the book. Even before that, though, his symbiotic intimacy with Orson surfaces in the scene in which Orestes overcomes Sandy's reticence and the two join in a Greek dance. Each must lift the other as part of the dance, and although Sandy believes at first that he cannot do it, he discovers ecstatically that he "can dance under his brother's weight" (72). The erotic overtones which reflect the intensity of the bond between Sandy and Orestes are an important, if provocative, part of Merrill's portrait of brotherhood.

In his notes for *The (Diblos) Notebook* Merrill wrote of Sandy that what "he must face in *his heart* is that he and Orestes are one."[11] The particulars of the book make it evident that what he meant was not that the brothers have identical or even similar natures but that they represent two halves of a single life, each feeling incomplete without the other and each somehow dependent on the other for happiness. The two halves of the relationship between the narrator and Orson have been kept separate by the narrator's guilt about his own fortunate circumstances in comparison with his brother's upbringing. Subconsciously postulating resentment on his brother's part, he converts him in the inset novel into a Romantic egoist who is unappealing enough to justify Sandy's coldness to him.

The narrator's depiction of Orestes as a Romantic egoist is in fact a compensatory reaction to his sense of his own ineffectualness. That sense of ineffectualness is presented in his novel, however, in the positive form of psychological refinement. The different viewpoints and temperaments of Sandy and Orestes are pointed up in their varying reactions to the Impressionistic paintings done by Dora's husband, Tasso. Sandy is moved by the delicate shades of the paintings, but Orestes cannot see it: "Orestes cannot understand why his brother is so touched by them—his own tastes run to Michelangelo, Grunewald, the monumental, the metaphysical" (36).

The portrayal of Orestes as a Romantic egoist is a mean between the narrator's polarized view of him as epic hero on the one hand and neurotic American tourist on the other. As an epic figure, Orestes is a projection of the narrator's hunger for heroism, which comes out during the outdoor staging of the ancient Greek plays at Epidauros. The actors strike him as like a "ballet of fleas on a round, lamplit table. When the gods finally came, I wanted them to be 40 feet tall" (25). While the narrator sees all too clearly, therefore, the tempestuous subjectivity of Orestes, for whom life *is* myth, he is also attracted to the residual power that clings to his portrayal of his brother.

Ironically, in shutting himself off from Orson's love, the narrator cripples his capacity to become attached to others, as is evident in his ill-starred relationship with the Americal girl, Lucine. That he feels his brother's love tugging at him, though, is indicated in his characterization of Sandy: "What Sandy hasn't known is how much he means to Orestes, & always has meant. O.: 'This is what I most regret about being so much older. Missing you, missing your childhood'" (60).

What breaks the logjam is the whipping that Byron administers to Orson, a humiliation that suddenly exposes Orson's vulnerability and need for love, thereby providing a basis on which the narrator can finally unite with him: "I turned to him now, arms open. We said each other's names & embraced. 'This is what I meant in my letter,' he said, stepping back, hands still on my shoulders. 'What I have wanted & never had from you.' Part of me," the narrator adds, "is still glowing with pleasure at those words. Part of me is still running away from them" (141). The ever-shifting visions and revisions of *The (Diblos) Notebook,* which are linked in part to the narrator's shadowboxing with his fictional characters and their 'real' prototypes, culminate in his perception that he himself has been the central, volatile, imponderable figure in his projected novel.

The multiplicity of viewpoints in *The (Diblos) Notebook* reflects Merrill's prismatic structuring. He described the technique in his notes as a "constantly shifting presentation of effects + motives, through which a light slowly dawns."[12] The deletions also produce an effect of gradual illumination. The deleted words, still visible beneath canceling, black lines, reveal original impulses which have been discarded for a variety of reasons. Merrill visualized the reader's eye as flying to the crossed-out words, which would seem to promise so much more than those left exposed. The device invites the reader to compare and decide for himself about variant readings, all the while becoming aware of the significance of the variants in the lives of the characters. Early in the novel, for example, a deletion reveals the narrator's buried feelings about Lucine: "I've seen L. off on the caïque. Her face in moonlight, gray & mild, as if about to ~~administer~~ receive an anesthetic" (33). The narrator's discomfort at Lucine's interest in him leads him to initially portray her as administering the anesthetic. A softening occurs as, aware of her confusion due to his coldness, he imagines her as submitting to the anesthetic.

The erratic typography and staccato pace of the *Notebook* tend to slow the reader down, forcing him to pause and consider the ambiguities of the text and to finish the uncompleted sentences and fragments for himself. Paradoxically, the "fair copy" of the projected novel looks rather flat in comparison with the earlier drafts. At one point, for example, the narrator describes Orestes as so addicted to Platonism that he is like the "oyster who can't feel the grit for the pearl." He revises this to read that Orestes "loses faith in phenomena uncolored by the imagination's powerful dyes" (80). Typically, the revision offers greater precision in meaning, but is also blander and more abstract than the original.

Merrill's major reservation about *The (Diblos) Notebook* was his fear that the novel's experimental ingenuity might be insufficiently related to its human drama.[13] Another way of seeing the potential difficulty is to consider whether or not the novel's technical innovations seduce the reader's attention away from the tale of the brothers. As has been demonstrated, though, form and theme reflect each other faithfully, much as the blue surface of the Aegean mirrors the Sleeping Woman of Troezen. *The (Diblos) Notebook* is an extraordinary work by any standard. Along with its brilliance in form, it offers a subtle and probing portrait of fraternal relationships that does much to meet Merrill's ambitious hopes for the book. Nevertheless, *Diblos* was to be his last completed novel. Increasingly, he came to feel in the 1960s that prose "feeds into poetry much more than the reverse."[14]

Chapter Four
Poems of the 1940s and 1950s
Jim's Book and *The Black Swan*

Jim's Book (1942) was privately printed when Merrill was 16. Along
with Frederick Buechner he had been active on the Lawrenceville
literary magazine, and the poems, essays, and narrative sketches in *Jim's
Book* were an outgrowth of that activity. While the book is ingenuous
and mannered, it does reveal Merrill's predilection for intricacy. The
poems use traditional meters while the stories, such as "Madonna,"
show the influence of well-established writers like Henry James. An
appreciative essay on Elinor Wylie shows her effect on his early work,
especially his attraction to melody and fancy.

The Black Swan (1946) was also privately printed, but Merrill
thought enough of these poems to include most of them in the first
trade edition of his poetry in 1951. The collection shows a Keatsian
interest in art and mutability, but even more apparent is the influence
of Wallace Stevens. "Medusa" which describes a worn, sculptured face
on a public fountain in autumn, is a good example:

> Birds and their songs were false
> As all imperishables,
> As the stone mask itself, its parables
> Of wingèd-heeled assassins, mirror-armed:
> For, to believe this face, it must be dreamed. (25)[1]

The stone mask is taken from Stevens's *Note Toward a Supreme Fiction,*
and the influence of his thought can be seen in the paradoxical relationship between dream and reality.

Stevens's presence can also be felt in *The Black Swan*'s emphasis on
perception and nominalism, especially in those poems which focus
explicitly on the eye. "The Green Eye" plays on Marvell's green
thought in a green shade motif, and, as with a number of these poems,

exhibits Merrill's fondness for the metaphysical conceit. The poem departs from artificial conventions, however, in focusing suddenly and almost with relief on the real experience of a saddened child:

> When here you bring your earliest tragedy,
> Your goldfish upside-down and rigidly
> Floating on weeds in the aquarium,
> Green is no panorama for your grief. (15)

"Perspectives of a Lonesome Eye" is a variation on the sestina, and thus gave Merrill an opportunity to pursue his interest in intricate form. The poem depicts the interlocked perspectives of an adult observer who is accustomed to manipulating his perceptions and that of the child within the adult with its lonesome, fearful, and primitive impressions of the world around it. On one level the opposed perspectives become imprisoning, perceptual tracks, causing a dissociation that, as always in Merrill, can only be overcome by love: "Bound by perspectives, we are loosed by love" (18). The reconciling of the poem's opposed perspectives also occurs within artists like the French pointillists who depict the "primitive / Sensation with lucidity that a child / Could understand" (17). Art thus parallels love's ability to bring harmony to the mind's and life's perplexing dualism.

"The Cosmological Eye" is another study in perspective, an exploration of how the eye's focusing on either foreground or background causes an inevitable blurring in the unfocused area. The feeling of melancholy at what is missed is balanced, however, by a paradoxical awareness of what is achieved. Thus, the observer in the poem takes pleasure in the "rare *azur*" of the "flawless" sky, drawing consolation from his consciousness that "happily blurred blue is no whit / Less exquisite than blue unblurred" (16). Characteristically, in these early poems the sky is visualized as both mirror and lens, like the eye which scans it. The poems delicately trace the play of light over the membrane of the eye—as in "From Morning Into Morning," where "each fixed moment" is caught by "blue refractions" (10).

The title poem, "The Black Swan," is represented on the book's cover by a swan looking at its mirrored image on the surface of a pond. Rather than being a natural creature, the bird is a point of departure for a studied arrangement of colors. Blackness stands for the hidden, fearful energies of the subconscious and the unknown while white symbolizes the open, inquiring light of consciousness, represented in the poem by the blond child on the shore. The child's love for the swan affirms the need for both darkness and light. Merrill sensitively explores the enhancement of consciousness by darkness by depicting the ceaseless movement of change and anguish across it and by showing the breaking up of its illusions under the impact of fresh experience.

"The Broken Bowl" offers yet another perspective on light and perception. The broken shards of a crystal bowl become prismatic reflectors which paradoxically give rise to a more complex and stimulating beauty than the intact bowl's "diehard brilliance" (9). The theme is that of a sort of fortunate fall in the world of perception. Freed from the "lucid unities" of their unshattered or unfallen state, the bowl's crystal fragments "triumph" like "love," building their harmonies from "dissonance" (9). Typical of the poems in *The Black Swan,* "The Broken Bowl" brushes against emotional experience without coming to rest in it. The reason is that Merrill's prior interest lay in his sense of the poem as visual artifact.

It might be argued in fact that emotion in *The Black Swan* issues from Merrill's appreciation for form. This can be seen, for example, in "The Formal Lovers":

> Like a Mondrian the windowframe
> Restricts the room and tells the lovers
> They must be still, let light be firm
> In gold geometry, subject their favors
> To a fevered dominance of form. (21)

Love grows in the reflexive consciousness of the lover, which gives it a definitive shape and captures its flow in a "stroke of bronze" (22).

Merrill had been influenced by Auden's *The Sea and the Mirror* (1944), and incorporated the two symbols of Auden's title in *The Black Swan.* While the mirror imagery is related to the mind, as has been seen, the sea is generally associated with the raw flux of life, the "broad, unbleached experience," as Merrill put it in "The Cosmological Eye" (16). In "Accumulations of the Sea," a symbolist poem, he depicts the sea as the neutral matrix of that which is overwhelming in our experience—time, erosion, death. The poem opens with the skeleton of a hand being carried by the sea onto the shore. The hand—

> Falls on grey sand, yet stencilled in its fall
> Against a band of ocean flaked with sunlight
> Touches at last the sand, as one descending
> The spiral staircase of association
> Around the well of substance. (12)

The mind, a Cubist "staircase of association," feels its essential weakness (if also its virtuosity) alongside nature, which appears to give life only to take it away. In this connection the skeleton of the hand metamorphoses into the skeleton of the past in a poignant emblem of loss:

> We watch the skeletons of childhood sunken
> In sockets of the beach, oyster-white bone,
> Stone, shell, sophistications of nostalgia,
> A music as of time on the victrola. (13)

The equivocal unity of man and nature is expressed in the images of the "pebbled eye" and the "pearled illusion in the ear" (13). The equivocation rests on the alternating triumphs of nature over man through death and loss and on the subtler evasions of these defeats by means of man's ability to assimilate nature through eye and mind. Merrill captures the stalemate incisively in the concluding stanza:

> But at the moment of annihilations,
> Unmoved by laughter or the whip of wings,
> Under the violent eyelid, the black sun
> For all its distance burns with a rose of blood. (14)

In the last analysis the mind must turn to the sea for everything it needs, for experience, meaning, even for mysticism. Thus, the swimmers in "Accumulations of the Sea" dive to "invisible shores" where the "coldest darkness sprouts" (13). Rising from these depths, they "plummet upward, leap half out of the sea / To greet with waterfall eyes the gentle air" (13). Like the sea, the waterfall is a ubiquitous symbol in Merrill, usually representing hidden, ineffable truth.

Technically, much of the writing in *The Black Swan* shows the influence of Hart Crane—as in "Phenomenal Love Song," with its arresting, violently compressed images. Merrill's interest in surrealism springs from his sense of it as a visual equivalent for word play, of which there is a good deal in *The Black Swan*. Rhyming puns combine with an elaborate, serpentine syntax to hold the reader's mind taut throughout. The book was a true beginning, and much that is characteristic of Merrill's work can be seen in it.

First Poems

The first trade edition of Merrill's poems, containing some of the poems from *The Black Swan* as well as many new pieces, came out in 1951. The lacquered workmanship of the collection led Howard Nemerov to remark waggishly at the time that Merrill's *First Poems* were "certainly very good for first poems; probably some of them would do even for second poems."[2] The poems deal with carefully distanced objects—a kite, a pelican, a willow tree—as if the only rationale for their existence were to nourish the spectator's consciousness and sensibility. Embellished with refined decorative flourishes, the poems celebrate the creative hush of the attentive mind. In terms of form the poems show Merrill's mastery over several traditional modes, from sonnets ("Procession") to sustained couplets ("Poem in Spring"), triplets ("Primer"), and terza rima ("Transfigured Bird").

Poised and impeccably phrased for the most part, the poems suffer from a certain coolness and dryness. The use of pronouns like "you" and "one" contributes to the overall mood of formalism as does the focus on universal subjects that appear to have been stripped of their local and personal details. Occasionally, a fresh, enlivening image from experience cuts through the ornate stillness of the verse, as with the picture of the playing children within the walled garden in "Wreath for the Warm-Eyed":

> Here children run
> Among the blossoms, pointing, calling,
> Each with his toy behind him trailing,
> A deformity worshipped, an introduction to pain. (25)[3]

The image both breathes life into the poem and enhances its symbolism since the trailing toy is a tiny presage of the child's fate.

In an effort to give vitality to his poems about perception, Merrill counted on his imagery to see him through. An example is "Foliage of

Vision," which superimposes the color and movement of the natural world on the otherwise abstruse materials of the poem. Thus, the "act by which we see" is depicted as both the "landscape-gardening of our dream / And the root's long revel under the clipped lawn" (39). The speaker wants to use appearances not to seek reality but to find palpable evidence for his preconceptions and dreams. The external world presses inexorably in on him, though, with its own statement of reality— "bird, fruit, wasp, limber vine, / Time and disaster and the limping blood" (40). Typical of *First Poems*, "Foliage of Vision" reflects a fastidious attention to both imagery and sound as can be seen in the subtle, internal rhyming on "plumb" and "thumb" in the third stanza.

In spite of Merrill's obvious care in structuring, most of these early poems are memorable not because of their overall designs but rather because of their individual details—such as the face of the parrot with its "haggard eye set in white crinkled paint" (50), the peacock, "Tense with idlesse" (54), and the pelican, a "Squatter on water" (52). "Transfigured Bird" is one of the more successful poems in a structural sense skillfully combining visual artifice, metaphysics, and narrative. The poem, a sustained display of terza rima, deals with a child's discovery of mortality after coming upon a broken eggshell that contains the embryo of a robin, frozen in death. Merrill records the scarring effects of the experience on the child's mind—"how there should be nothing cleanly for years to come, / Nor godly, nor reasons found, nor prayers spoken" (49). The poem contains other kinds of birds as well, however, including Yeats's golden Byzantine bird and Fabergé's exquisitely jeweled birds. These birds of art emphasize survival in another form, thereby offsetting the oppressive mood of mortality in the poem. In retrospect, the reader sees that the images have been neatly polarized throughout the poem, as in the "point of blood" in the "fertile yolk" in the second section (46).

First Poems contains Merrill's first, noteworthy experiments in the long poem. The variations format, which like much of Merrill's structuring, was derived from music, allowed him to pursue different verse forms within a single thematic framework. The six sections of "The Air is Sweetest that a Thistle Guards" constitute six, distinct movements grouped around the motifs of the title, which dialectically pairs the themes of danger and pleasure, finiteness and release. The first poem is a tapestry which shows the aesthetic significance of air as a creature with force and movement. Air materializes, as it were, in passing through the thistle like wind shuttling over the tops of sea waves "taut between those waters and these words, / Our air, our morning, the poignant thistles weave / Nets that bind back, garland the hungering wave" (27).

There is a shift in mood in the second poem as the thistle is depicted as a spiky "mullein-leaf," and is later associated with the "cactus and yucca, the moral thorn that only / A snail can master" (27). The jab of pain is as pronounced here as the sough of pleasure had been in the first poem. In the third poem, which is written in a lively dimeter with humorous feminine rhymes, the image of the thistle becomes part of a fanciful motif. At first the poem resembles a fairy tale ("Flowers are people / Enchanted by witches"), but then darkens toward the end into a sardonic fable:

> . . . people are flowers.
> They fall helter-skelter
> In their first witching weather
> Or turn wry like thistles
> Who, bristling together,
> Brag of their shelters,
> Insist that each latest
> is safest, sweetest. (28)

The fourth poem, set in a modified ottava rima, is a desultory narrative about love and loss, and is the least successful of the variations. The poem teaches among other lessons that one cannot immunize oneself against pain by preparing for it. In the fifth poem Merrill creates a historic setting in which to set forth his central motifs. In 1077 the Holy Roman emperor, Henry II, stood barefoot in the snow at Canossa for three days before receiving the Pope's pardon for having attempted to conquer Italy. The mood of the variation is penitential and submissive, its imagery chastening and faintly mystical. Here the thistle, which had earlier been a source of torment, brings about the refinement of the soul.

Appropriately, the sixth and final poem opens with a sense of freshness and renewal that is reflected in the colloquial phrasing and rhythms as well as in the speaker's presence, which in turn gives the poem a welcome feeling of immediacy:

> Friday, Clear. Cool. This is your day. Stendhal
> At breakfast-time. The metaphors of love.

> Lucky, perhaps, big Beyle, for whom love was
> So frankly the highest good, to be garlanded
> Accordingly, without oblivion, without cure. (32)

Stendhal's *De L'amour* (1822) was a frank, psychological analysis of love that anticipated the writings of Freud. Like the fragrant air around the thistle and like the pearl that grew from irritation (poem five) love is pictured as swelling around a "small unlovely need" (32). Enhanced by the conversational ease of the blank verse, the focus in the sixth poem on the life of a real protagonist gives the sequence a final feeling of liberation—as if one had moved suddenly from the closed room of thought outside into the flow of life.

"Variations and Elegy: White Stag, Black Bear" is dedicated to Merrill's father on whose ring were the carved figures of a "black bear and milk-white stag / In mortal conflict" (58). The design is a dualistic tableau of warring impulses both in Merrill's father and within nature in general. In the second poem the two animals are submerged in a zoo motif in which the seven deadly sins are related to different animals. The poem ends with a seriocomic view of Merrill's father, who is pictured as depleted by a life of excess: "To a tired man, winter / Recommends the bear" (58).

Poems three and four also center allegorically on the bear and deer motifs. The sensual man (the bear) finds his life complicated by the uninvited but inextricable presence of "spirit" (the deer), which paradoxically loomed "where most we saw / Body: wonderful shapes in the white air / Transfigured Bruin" (59). Ironically, the soul shows itself unexpectedly more durable than the body in the hunting scene that dominates poem four:

> Hunters choke the golden clearing
> With apertures: eye, nostril, ear: for there
> The white stag prances, unicorn-rare
> Whose hooves since dawn were steering
> His captors toward beatitude. (59)

Poem five offers a symbolistic reading of the black and white design of the ring. In addition, the soul is urged to transcend its narrow attachment to sensual beauty:

All you who lie in the black night,
Blacker than flesh in darkness, never
Inspired to tell love from lover,
How far the flesh past touch and sight
Moves in its felicity
You shall never understand,
Until the leper says (your hand
Resting in his white hand) Kiss me. (60)

The sixth poem describes the marriage of body and soul. Because each keeps its narrow perspective of the other, however, the relationship founders, the stag goring the bear while the bear sinks its teeth into the stag's shoulder. Significantly, the white stag, which had appeared as the inevitable victim at the outset of the poem, is dominant here, requiring of the "veined black stone on which he stands / Reflection into flesh" (62).

The variations conclude with an "Elegy," which initially appears to revert to the defeatism of the second poem. The autumnal scene with its blood-red colors conveys the sense of the body's gradual retreat, and is here associated with the ailments of Merrill's father. The red hues symbolize feeling while black and white stand for a more distanced perspective on the human condition. The mood softens as the poem focuses on the scene of a bear gorging himself on honey in the fall. Merrill then skillfully unites the figures of winter, the white stag, and the bear in the image of a snow-covered bear, an emblem of the body's final sleep, a body which is now, however, fully possessed of a soul. The final confrontation of the hunters and the white bear has the connotations of an epic meeting. Significantly, the hunters are unable to say which "beast they chased," deer or bear, soul or body (66). "White Stag, Black Bear" is one of the most powerful and evocative poems ever written by Merrill, ironically included in a collection that otherwise seems somewhat effete.

Although the pieces in *First Poems* rarely touch on autobiographical sources—"White Stag, Black Bear" being an eloquent exception—Merrill does introduce his readers to Charles. He thought of Charles as a projection of himself, "slightly more mature, slightly more even tempered, slightly more worldly" than he was when he wrote the half-dozen poems about Charles in the 1950s and 1960s.[4] Charles provides an elegant, urbane, faintly droll narrative presence and a fresh source of animation for Merrill's otherwise frozen landscapes. In "River Poem," for example, Charles catalytically animates the still-life figures used to symbolize the theme of perceptual relativism. The poem also gains immediacy from the fluency of its blank verse.

Other poems that Merrill has identified as having autobiographical significance are "Willow" and "The House." They are formal poems (both done in triplets), and Merrill recalls that " 'Real' experience had graced them, somehow."[5] "The House" is the more important of the two, since houses are a seminal symbol in Merrill's work. The house in the poem is as vulnerable as those who sleep within it, its west walls taking the "sunset like a blow" (71). Wind, rain, and darkness swirl so that the house appears finally to be as naked as the grave. The wildness of the elements without is paralleled by the troubling dreams of the speakers within. Softly, Merrill approaches the "wet-faced sleepers the winds take / To heart" in a moment that both captures his own bottomless loneliness and his recognition of the insecurity of all men (72). "The House" is one of the few moving poems in the collection. Perhaps by reason of their formal excellence, most of the poems in *First Poems* cry out for subjects worthy of their finely wrought styles.

Short Stories

In spite of its title, *Short Stories* (1954) is a slim volume of poetry which was brought out by a small New England press. Circulation of the book was limited, and most of the poems were reprinted in the later, more widely distributed *Country of a Thousand Years of Peace* (1959). In many respects the poems in *Short Stories* represent a perceptible advance over the spaceless and timeless *First Poems*. Some of the poems *are* short stories, and represented Merrill's attempt to revive a narrative tradition that had been ignored by the contemporary emphasis on the lyric. Some, like "A Narrow Escape," are witty parodies of novelistic forms. Others, like "The Octopus" and "Midas Among Goldenrod," are given a narrative coloring. The poems are generally written in blank verse, giving Merrill the flexibility he needed to sustain the flow of voice and incident. In this connection he has said: "I wanted to write blank verse—even before I wrote the poems. Why? Because I wanted to get some of the pleasures of prose into poetry."[6]

Nonetheless, he never did let go of rhyme completely, and intermittent rhymes show up in poems like "The Cruise."

"The Cruise" is about well-to-do passengers on a transatlantic ocean liner which suddenly encounters an iceberg. A child ("little Agnes") cries out at the sight of it, but the narrator and her adult companions go on with their talk, apparently unconscious of and indifferent to the iceberg's "brilliant fraction and, wakeful beneath, / That law of which nine-tenths is a possession / By powers we do not ourselves possess" (3).[7] Later, in a foreign souvenir shop the narrator comes across some monstrous-looking crystal figures which, like the iceberg, are connected with the ocean. A professor traveling with the narrator describes the figures as archaic "nightmares" that had at one time "set aswirl the mind of China" (4). The figures are pictured as "fawning / On lengths of ocean-green brocade," tamed by the imagination of the artist and by the process of art itself (4). The narrator wonders, however: "Are we less monstrous when our motive slumbers / Drugged by a perfection of our form?" (4). She purchases one of the figures, placing it on a lower shelf after her return in order to remind herself dimly of her encounter with darkness. "The Cruise" is both dense and pliable, given weight by its fearful themes and yet held up by the pluckiness of its narrator.

In "Gothic Novel" the daughter of an Italian count discovers a secret doorway behind a wall. She starts down the dark stairway, suddenly tempted by a rush of murderous thoughts about her husband whose body she imagines concealing in the secret passageway. She gradually abandons these thoughts, inhibited by the guilty realization that she would have to justify the act in time—both to others and herself. She seals the door up, and retreats back into the cramped confines of her marriage. On one level her wild thoughts have merely been a change of pace, "Infant alternatives to the workaday" (1). On another level the episode has been a crucial, terrifying moment of choice, a choice that leads to her becoming a "matron, suddenly"—

> Become, in short, a life, a trodden path.
> Dazzle of choice, anon there shall be none:
> The candle gutters at a breath, her own.
> Put down the book unread. The tale is done. (1–2)

The equivocation in the final lines, in which one is uncertain whether the tale is real or merely something that the *contessina* has been reading, underlines the gap between Gothic fiction and actual life. At the same time, the bleak dissatisfaction of the woman's life engenders a genuine pathos in the poem.

"A Narrow Escape" contains all of the ingredients of a Gothic potboiler. The tautness of the poem comes from the incongruity between its jaded, gossipy surface and the occult darkness of its contents. Merrill has always been fond of playing off such differences of texture and subject matter against each other in order to create brittleness. Here, though, the tension is drolly mitigated by the parodied, tired conventions of the Dracula story. "A View of the Burning," another Gothic tale, is based on the execution of Cardinal Wolsey by Henry VIII. The poem's force derives from the fact that the story of Wolsey, "crimson" in his cardinal's robes even before he submits to the flames, is told from Henry's unrepentant viewpoint. The surface of the poem is alive with the sort of witty luminescence that one might find in a comedy of manners while the grisly nature of the action throws the poem into shock. The tonal lightness begins with Henry's initial mention of Wolsey in which he reveals his callous awareness of Wolsey's innocence: "Righteous or not, here comes an angry man" (2). The poem is a brilliant miniature of a decadent and lascivious king who, aware of the fear of heaven that paralyzes others, looks to no power beyond himself.

While not, strictly speaking, a story, "Midas Among Goldenrod" does contain a droll narrative situation. The Phrygian king of the Greek myth whose touch turned everything to gold is here appropriately surrounded by it in the form of a field of goldenrod. The problem is that the golden flowers bring out his hay fever—a lightly textured, contemporary version of Midas's traumatic aversion to gold in the original myth. In the poem Merrill pays playful homage to the blemish in every near-perfect situation, the "sly / Irritant in the gold of an environment" (9). The poem is a refreshing antidote to his earlier, introspective studies with its cheerful statement about the impact and impartiality of the external world, a mild rebuke of those who "believe that only / The mind suffers" (9).

"The Octopus," "The Wintering Weeds," "About the Phoenix," and "The Greenhouse" are emblematic studies reminiscent of Merrill's *First Poems*. Some of them exhibit a new narrative embroidery, as in "The Wintering Weeds" where the initial excitement of a first snowfall is followed by feelings of weariness as winter settles in. The transition in feeling is arrestingly visualized in terms of a "rich woman weary of a young man / Who bites his lip till it is numb with shame / Less for his soiling suit than her deceit" (5). "About the Phoenix" deals with man's fluctuating hope in immortality. The speaker's wavering speculations conclude with a belief in a "mortal lull," an afterglow in which the luminous faces of the dead flicker in the mind before being permanently snuffed out:

> And dawn, discovering ashes not yet stirred,
> Buildings in rain, but set on rock,
> Beggars and sparrows entertaining one another,
> Showed me your face, for that moment neither
> Alive nor dead, but turned in sleep
> Away from whatever waited to be endured. (8)

Apart from its evocative imagery and imaginative cosmology, the poem is enlivened by the countervailing play of voice amidst its dire speculations—as in the tone of ennui in the opening line: "But in the end one tires of the high-flown" (6).

"About the Phoenix," like most of the poems in *Short Stories,* is elliptical and subtle, perhaps overly so for the tradition of the short story. Nonetheless, the poems in this collection bristle with narrative surprises and incongruities as short stories have a habit of doing. Moreover, while Merrill's elongated syntax has doubtlessly proved frustrating to some readers, it harbors in its turning clauses and phrases those unexpected shadings and unlooked for ironies that make the difference between a flat and an absorbing tale. In any case, from *Short Stories* on, narrative was to become a fixed and honored part of Merrill's poetic practice.

The Country of a Thousand Years of Peace

In addition to those poems reprinted from *Short Stories, The Country of a Thousand Years of Peace* (1959) contained new poems that can be distinguished from Merrill's earlier work by their greater depth and tightened form. The poems record Merrill's extensive traveling during the 1950s which, in the case of cities like Amsterdam, evidently left its scars. Many of the poems recount the experience of the heart—as opposed to the detachment of the earlier contemplative studies. Nevertheless, Merrill's attachment to metaphysical poetry carries through in poems like "The Lovers." The poem, Merrill recalls, was "one of a great number of my poems where the human situation *is* a metaphor or perhaps even a vision."[8] The central conceit involves an elaborate, homely comparison between lovers' caresses and the hands of a farmer who washes up in the open at the end of the day. The initial absurdity of the comparison is overcome as the poem focuses exquisitely on the reflection of the setting sun on the water in the open-air basin, transfiguring the farmer, the world around him, and, by extension, the lovers into gold leaf.

A number of the poems have to do with mirrors. As opposed to the earnest, epistemological analysis that accompanied the mirror motif in the earlier poems, however, these poems open onto narrative and myth. The result is that there is more action in the poems in *The Country of a Thousand Years of Peace* than in earlier volumes. In "Mirror," for example, the speaker is a large looking-glass that has witnessed a family's history, and tells about it. The mirror's pride at being the family historian is offset by an innate imperfection in its way of reflecting reality—its flat surface. The mirror literally lacks perspective, and this is reflected in its indiscriminate, if attentive, recording of events. Because Merrill explores his epistemological themes within the framework of the dramatic monologue, the poem's center of gravity shifts from these themes to the plight of the abandoned mirror, which with disuse lapses into shabbiness, waiting for its remaining silver

> To blister, flake, float leaf by life, each milling-
> Downward dumb conceit, to a standstill
> From which not even you strike any brilliant
> Chord in me, and to a faceless will,
> Echo of mine, I am amenable.

"In the Hall of Mirrors," which is set at Versailles, deals with the difference between a two-dimensional and three-dimensional reflection of reality. The man and woman who are escorted through the hall of mirrors reject it as "Complex but unmysterious" after witnessing the breathtaking reflections produced by the magnificent branching chandeliers. The poem ends with their departure and a return to the crystalline stillness of the hall, now felt, though, to be frigidly incomplete without its guests: "From glass to glass an interval / Widens like

moonrise over frost / No tracks have ever crossed" (76). Merrill intended the poem to have mythic significance, saying that it is about the
"expulsion from Eden."[9] His remark is consistent with the poem's
turning toward the warmth of experience away from the virginal beauty
of the hall of mirrors. He himself appeared in fact to be gradually
moving away from a preoccupation with perception and artifice toward
the roundedness of actual experience.

The camera, a variation on the mirror motif, is taken up in "Some
Negatives: X. at the Chateau." Once again, Merrill explores the
contrast between the surfaces of form and the depths of experience. In
this connection the speaker remarks at one point that "no image sinks to
truth" (14). The photographic negative of the visit to the chateau,
unlike a flat, mirrorlike print, releases the imagination by transforming
the quiet girl in the picture into an exotic negress. In addition, the
tranquil background becomes wild with "thunderous" skies and a
"cypress walk / Copied in snow" (13). The negative permits the speaker
to visualize the girl as she never was, altering her "simple diffidence" to
a fiery eroticism that in the scenario suggested by the negative might
have led to the sensationalism of "lake, lawn, urn and maze / Plotted by
your dead rivals with no care / That I should love you next" (13). Once
again, the narrative setting anchors the action in the speaker, whose
perceptual themes, interesting enough in themselves, become all the
more engrossing when set within the context of his life and feelings.

A number of poems in *The Country of a Thousand Years of Peace* are
about nature, and here as well there is a change in direction, although
poems like "The Locusts" and "Thistledown" recall Merrill's earlier
work. "Fire Poem" in particular reveals a change in the role of nature
from that of a spectatorial field for the eye to an autonomous, powerful
entity in its own right. As a monologue in which fire speaks to man, the
poem anticipates the style of *Braving the Elements* (1972). Here, the
hypnotic beauty of the fire is indissolubly connected with its danger,
the two joined in the veiled image of the phoenix—the *"rare bird bedded
at the heart of harm"* (4). "The Dunes" is a celebration of nature's power.
Whipped into a "makeshift" form of existence by strong shore winds,
the shifting dunes, ostensibly worthless and tentative, evoke in the
speaker a joyful sense of being: "To have a self, even of salt and sand!"
(32)

Increasingly, Merrill portrayed man *in* nature and aware of his
continuity with nature. In "A Renewal," for example, autumnal winds

resolve a standoff between the two lovers in the poem, abruptly reminding them of how little time they have left:

> Having used every subterfuge
> To shake you, lies, fatigue, or even that of passion,
> Now I see no way but a clear break.
> I add that I am willing to bear the guilt.
>
> You nod assent. Autumn turns windy, huge,
> A clear vase of dry leaves vibrating on and on.
> We sit, watching. When I next speak
> Love buries itself in me, up to the hilt. (15)

Significantly, the speaker is affected not so much by autumn's chill as by its "huge" presence. Nature gives perspective to man's situation instead of the other way around as had been the case in many of the earlier poems.

A good number of the poems in *The Country of a Thousand Years of Peace* have to do with myths or dreams. Both provided Merrill with a way of relating the imagination to nature while retaining the concreteness of a narrative framework. Nature could be perceived both in picturesque, naturalistic detail and as an emblem of cosmic order. "Olive Grove," written in Merrill's favorite quatrains, deals with the myth of creation. Athena, daughter of Zeus, is pictured as having created a primordial olive tree out of the rocks just as the dreamer in the poem creates a new world out of the union of his unconscious mind and his rustic surroundings. The poem's delicately extended thread (it is a single sentence) draws together the motifs of ancient myth and the images of contemporary Greece into a vivid synthesis of universal archetypes.

"Three Sketches for Europa" exhibits a similar montage of myth and actuality. The first poem, a sonnet, depicts an American tourist's patronizing view of war-torn Europe. The poem describes the allegorical journey of a young man on a visit to his European grandmother, who, like Europe itself, had been a cultured beauty but had become "peevish now, an invalid" (46). The second poem, "Geography," a sonnet set in rhyming couplets, is a montage of the Greek myth of Zeus and Europa set over the map of Europe. In the myth Europa is raped by Zeus (in the shape of a bull), who carries her eastward over the Mediterranean, thereby completing the map of Europe. The poem ends with a brilliant pun in the superimposed images of Europa and Europe, now seen to be "no longer chaste but continent" (47).

"At the Bullfight," the final sketch, is a sonnet that continues the bull symbol, and adds the motif of the maze, which also derives from the story of Europa. Europa gave birth to Minos, the creator of the famous labyrinth of Crete. The minotaur, which lurked at the heart of the labyrinth, is also present in the poem ("Where the thing waits"). The major symbolism, however, centers on a bullfight and on Merrill's retelling of the myth in a revised version that involves Europa's seduction of Zeus. He pictures her hanging him with garlands and provocatively urging him "into the foam with gentle phrases" (48). The gory image of the dying bull and the motifs of the bullring and the labyrinth allegorically undercut the poem's mood of injured innocence and suggest a postwar Europe that had sunk into a demoralized hedonism, forgetful of its heroic myths. Apart from the vividness and layered complexity of each of the three poems, Merrill's overlapping of motifs between and among them shows an impressive command of structuring.

"Salome," which deals with biblical myth, has three poetic movements with shared motifs, each of which presents a central character (John the Baptist, a mad dog, a mad scientist) who illustrates the theme that "you can have enough / Of human love" (30). Turning away from the hysterics of human history, the poem slopes finally with somber acceptance toward nature as the matrix of all experience— including the mind's: "Suns lighten and winds whirl / Back into earth, the easier school" (31). While it also deals with mythic archetypes, "Dream (Escape from the Sculpture Museum) and Waking" introduces some autobiographical materials so that here one has the sense that the dream is important not only in a symbolic sense but because it is Merrill's dream. In the opening scene of the dream snow unexpectedly begins to fall over the marble sculptures, and inside the dream the sleeping Merrill wonders why:

> Because of the statues perhaps.
> Or because for a long time now
> I have wanted to be more natural
> Than they. (66–67)

Merrill did indeed strive "to be more natural" in *The Country of a Thousand Years of Peace*. The naturalness came about through adjustments in form and through his greater openness about his own experience. Although some of the travel poems, "At Mamallapuram" and "Kyoto. At the Detached Palace," for example, are relatively impersonal, others, like "Hotel de l'Univers et Portugal," expose Merrill's vulnerable sense of dislocation as he moved about from country to country. Self-consciously aware of himself as one in a succession of nightly guests who have slept in the same bed, he reveals his unprotected feelings in a "strange city's clear grave acids" (17). Even more candid is "Amsterdam," which portrays the harrowing effect of the pursuit of sensuality, the anticipatory mounting of passion as the evening draws closer and the deadened, hallucinatory aftermath in the following day's sunshine.

Merrill's new openness is shown in his readiness to talk about his experience with spiritualism ("Voices from the Other World") and in his willingness to write about those who were close to him. The elegiac title poem, "The Country of a Thousand Years of Peace," is about Merrill's young, Dutch, poet friend, Hans Lodeizen, who died of leukemia in 1950. On one level the title reflects Switzerland's long-standing political neutrality, but it also points to the necropolis setting that generates the poem's emotion. Lodeizen was to become one of a half-dozen recurring characters who make up the human landscape of Merrill's poems. They become so familiar to the reader that their mere appearance in a poem by Merrill becomes instantly symbolic, evoking a voice, gestures, attitudes, and past scenes. Together, these figures constitute not only Merrill's experience and consciousness, but through a cumulative, Proustian imprinting they in fact *become* him.

Though Merrill's relationship with Hans Lodeizen was not always a smooth one—as he indicates in "The Book of Ephraim" (*Divine Comedies*, 56)—the death of the young man became rooted in his imagination. The slow, inexorable wasting away of Lodeizen as the disease took its course is captured in the title poem in the image of the sword that, dangling high above him, "never falling, kills" (2). The concluding poem in *The Country of a Thousand Years of Peace* is also dedicated to Lodeizen, and introduces a balancing note of consolation which hovers in the beauty of the moment that binds Merrill to his dead friend: "There are moments when speech is but a mouth pressed / Lightly and humbly against the angel's hand" (77).

In the same new spirit of openness Merrill wrote about members of his family—as in "A Timepiece," which is a study of his sister during pregnancy. Here, Merrill associates his central conceit—the

hourglass—with someone he cares about, giving the poem the emotional involvement that was often absent in the early metaphysical
poems. "A Timepiece" has the polish, craft, and descriptiveness of the
early poems together with a new directness, realism, and intimacy of
tone. The nine-month development of the unborn child, which slowly
shapes the woman's feelings into maternal ones, becomes associated
with the succession of the generations. As a result the palpitating new
life in Merrill's sister's womb simultaneously signals her own aging.
The infant produces a "striking in her breast, / For soon by what it tells
the clock is still" (8). The woman is an hourglass, then, not only
because of her swollen figure but because she symbolizes the span of
mortal life.

In addition to poems devoted to his family—such as "Upon a Second
Marriage," a dignified lyric addressed to his mother—Merrill wrote
poems about the quotidian details that made up much of his life. The
poem "Three Chores" is a good example, with its mundane subtitles—
"Water Boiling," "Night Laundry," and "Italian Lesson." In these
poetic sketches Merrill anchors himself in the concreteness of his daily
routine and then lets his imagination transform his ostensibly homely
subjects. "Night Laundry" is an especially successful example:

> A week of swans depending
> From wooden beaks take flight
> Flapping at dawn from water's
> Jewel of the first water
> And every dismal matter's
> Absorption in its cleansing
> Bring the new day to light. (43)

The metamorphosis of the laundry into the flight of swans and the
symbolic "Absorption" of the motif of the wash water by the morning
dew are characteristic of Merrill's heightening of the commonplace, his
ability to reveal beauty where none is expected. Similarly, "The Doodler" follows Merrill's scribblings on a telephone pad into the "white
void" of creation itself (53). "The Doodler" celebrates the mind, which
can make lasting beauty even out of its own boredom.

The Country of a Thousand Years of Peace exhibits a new and attractive
buoyancy, particularly conspicuous in poems like "Who Guessed

Amiss the Riddle of the Sphinx," which portrays the oddly exhilarating effect of a fallen tree on a child's imagination. The buoyancy is also visible in Merrill's exuberant use of word play. The most daring example is the pun on the word "heart" in "Laboratory Poem." Charles watches Naomi dissect live turtles in the laboratory in what turns out to be a severe test of their relationship. While his presence emotionally helps her to perform her gory experiments, the prognosis for the two of them is not promising as he ponders the fate of human hearts that have climbed through "violence into exquisite disciplines / Of which, as it now appeared, they all expired" (41). The lines are typical of the best of Merrill's poems in the 1950s with their combination of surface finesse and underlying emotional rupture.

The Country of a Thousand Years of Peace is a watershed volume in Merrill's career. In the 1940s and 1950s he was in search of his *métier* as a poet and as a novelist and dramatist. These were years of apprenticeship in the traditional sense, a time in which one mastered a craft. The suppleness and fine glaze of Merrill's poetry were the result of a diligent attention to prosody and tone while he continued his search for themes. By the time he wrote *The Country of a Thousand Years of Peace,* he had settled on a subject—the self. Merrill chose the self not as hero or Romantic idealist but as the center of a domestic and uneventful life, the self that in spite of his all too evident culture and virtuosity bound him to the rest of mankind.

Chapter Five
The Middle Period

Water Street

The most noticeable difference between the poems in *Water Street* (1962) and Merrill's earlier work is the relaxed tone. The poems show him in a bemused but absorbed conversation with himself. He wrote the poems from the settled perspective of the house he shared with David Jackson in Stonington, Connecticut, the restive years in New York and the years of foreign travel now well behind him. He divided his time in the early 1960s between Athens and Connecticut, both of which provided him with a sense of rootedness. The title of *Water Street* conveys a fundamental sense of stability although a symbolic dualism underlies the Heraclitean polarization of water and street. The dualism reflects Merrill's benign consciousness of change at this period in his life through which he looks both wistfully back and hopefully ahead.

Merrill's sense of being in the midstream of his life is reflected in "The Water Hyacinth" where he paradoxically develops paternal feelings toward his aging and forgetful grandmother. The emotional balance is righted, however, when he considers the fullness of her experience in comparison with his own incomplete life:

> Your entire honeymoon,
> A ride in a rowboat
> On the St. Johns River,
> Took up an afternoon.
> And by that time, of course,
> The water hyacinth
> Had come here from Japan,
> A mauve and rootless guest
> Thirsty for life, afloat
> With you on the broad span
> It would in sixty years
> So vividly congest. (40)[1]

As the image of the congested water flowers implies, it is the very richness of his grandmother's experience that causes her memories and anecdotes to merge and perhaps to become confused at times as she grows old.

The poems in *Water Street* reflect a quiet joyfulness that is based in part on self-acceptance—as can be seen in "To a Butterfly":

> Goodness, how tired one grows
> Just looking through a prism:
> Allegory, symbolism.
> I've tried, Lord knows,
> To keep from seeing double,
> Blushed for whenever I did,
> Prayed like a boy my cheek be hid
> By manly stubble. (43)

The high spirits of some of the poems can be seen in the ebullient puns of "The Grand Canyon": "This first mistake / Made by your country is also / The most sublime" (14). The play on the canyon's geological "fault" is typical of the vivacity and humor of *Water Street*. Even in "The Parrot Fish," which depicts the slow dying of the caught fish, the final shudders are partially offset by the lesson learned and by Merrill's description of the gaudiness of the fish: "Chalk-violet, olive, all veils and sequins, a / Priestess out of the next Old Testament extravaganza" (45). Similarly, in "Prism," a glass paperweight rises to life with the coming of dawn when a "toneless waltz glints through the pea-sized funhouse. / The day is breaking someone else's heart" (17). The lift created by the pun on daybreak and heartbreak keeps the emotion afloat amidst the very real pain alluded to.

In spite of the continued facelessness of Merrill's lovers, which reflects his discreet reserve at this time, the poems are rich in feeling. "Poem of Summer's End" portrays a shared feeling of apprehension about the coming chill of fall, which is already felt in sky and air and which causes the lovers to turn inward, confident that "love is what they are and where they go" (11). In "Getting Through," the speaker's mounting frustrations at not being able to mail a love letter are warmly balanced by the underlying certainty of that love and by the thin but illuminative winter light that ends a day of strain and disappointment:

> The stationery store's brow drips, ablaze
> Where the pink sun has struck it with the hand
> Of one remembering after days and days—
> Remembering what? I am a fool, a fool!
> I hear with joy, helpless to understand
> Cries of snow-crimson children leaving school. (31)

The cries of the children and the light of the pale sun against the white background cathartically release the speaker from his own inner turmoil by showing him a picture of opposites in taut but satisfying equilibrium, an emblem of forbearance.

Some of the poems in *Water Street* are about the act of writing itself—or sometimes about Merrill's inability to write, as in "Angel." Writing represented a great deal of his experience, and so had a place in poetry that focused on daily experience. In "From a Notebook" the whiteness of snow falling outside merges with that of a notebook page. The oppressiveness of the scene is overcome by the writing of the first word which "stops / The blizzard" (7). After the page is filled, the blankness of Merrill's life has also, the poem implies, been filled in. Similarly, Merrill's poem "For Proust" celebrates the French writer's capacity to salvage fertile memories even from life's bitter disappointments, thereby transforming the flesh of the artist's face into a "thin gold mask" (19).

Merrill dwells further on the relationship between the artist and life in "Homunculus Artifex." The title refers to the alchemical homunculus, a legendary man-made humanoid. The "manikins" in the poem have a garden party in order to indulge their longing to be fully human:

> The ill-knit creatures, now in hues
> Of sunstroke, mulberry, white of clown,
> Yellow of bile, bruise-blacks-and-blues,
> Stumped outward, waving matchstick arms,
> Colliding, poking, hurt, in tears
> (For the wound became an eye)
> Toward the exciting, hostile greens
> And the spread cloths of Art. (25–26)

The affectiveness of the language signals the success of their brief sharing of humanity, like the artist's characters who in privileged moments manage to exceed their artificial natures.

Merrill's autobiographical gallery in *Water Street* includes two of his grandparents. "The Smile" is about his grandfather on his father's side who, according to Merrill, had a "silver plate in his skull, and died on our sleeping-porch in Palm Beach." The false teeth in the poem belong to Merrill's father, though, and recollections of his father's death as well as his grandfather's seep into the poem.[2] The simplicity of the poem's action—an old man moves slowly from his chair to his bed in order to sleep and to die—is mirrored in the unusual baldness of the language and syntax. Although the details are imagistically concrete, feeling rushes into the poem as the old man places his "round gold watch / Unwound, among / Dimes, quarters, lunatic change" on the dresser (48). The word "lunatic" releases the poem's emotion as Merrill reacts to the incongruity between the orderly chain of events that precedes the death and the death itself. The poem illustrates how firmly Merrill's poems, for all of their profusion of images, were now anchored in action. While not entirely giving up his penchant for tapestry, he had moved toward the nearer and warmer field of memory as his fundamental principle of design.

"Annie Hill's Grave" is about Merrill's grandmother on his mother's side. She had died in the early 1930s after also having lived with Merrill's family during his childhood years. The poem records Merrill's memory of her funeral and burial, events that became etched on his mind as a boy. Finally independent, the adult Merrill accompanies his grandmother to her grave in a tender reenactment of family history. Elegiac heightening can only sustain him so far, however, and he is left with the unsettling image of his grandmother in the ground where the "silence drums into her upturned face" (41). The poem's poignancy, which coexists with its unflinchingly unsentimental view of death, make it one of Merrill's most memorable poems.

Through cultivating an autobiographical art, Merrill was able to retain a narrative matrix for his poems while forsaking the fancifulness of some of his earlier work. "Scenes of Childhood" involves a screening of home movies by Merrill and his mother. The thirty-year-old pictures gradually reveal the young Merrill as having been at the center of an Oedipal drama. This is vividly apparent in his reaction to the shadow of his father across his mother's dress in one of the early family scenes:

> A quiet chuckle escapes
> My white-haired mother

> To see in that final light
> A man's shadow mount
> Her dress. And now she is
> Advancing, sister-
> less, but followed by
> A fair child, or fury—
> Myself at four, in tears.
> I raise my fist,
> Strike, she kneels down. The man's
> Shadow afflicts us both. (21)

The child's "fury" and the sexual overtones of his father's shadow constitute an emotional tinderbox whose effects reach into the present. The inflammatory nature of the filmed scene is symbolized by the film's catching fire when Merrill's mother, mesmerized by her past and by her husband once again, asks her son to slow the film down. The episode reveals Merrill's father, long after he had ceased to live with his wife and son, as a continuing emotional vortex in their lives.

In prosaic terms the portentous shadow of Merrill's father was probably caused by the fact that he took the pictures. As if in recognition of such calming realities, the poem settles toward the end. The Oedipal resonances added by the mind exhaust themselves eventually as Merrill considers his father's declining years. The later shrunken view of his father is associated with the image of the "skulls of flies," an image whose morbidness is offset by a vision of the stars as Merrill steps out under the night sky after the screening:

> Immensely still
> The heavens glisten. One broad
> Path of vague stars is floating
> Off, a shed skin
> Of all whose fine cold eyes
> First told us, locked in ours:
> You are the heroes without name
> Or origin. (24)

The poem yokes the simplified, heroic vision of the child with the belittling viewpoint of the adult in a final unresolvable tension. More important, perhaps, Merrill shows that the adult, for all of his irony, lives his life in the shadow of determinative, childhood experiences whose lifelong effect he comes to understand too late. It is this underlying recognition that gives the poem its essential power and helps to make it one of Merrill's finest.

"The World and the Child," an accomplished example of the villanelle, recalls Merrill's experience as a sick child having been put to bed in an upstairs bedroom while his parents entertained below. Lying awake in the gray dark, the child contemplates his loneliness, his need to be comforted by parents whose attention is elsewhere. The pathos of the situation is held in check by the conspicuousness of the poem's form, especially through the recurring rhymes. The use of enclosed forms to modulate emotion is typical of the poems of Merrill's middle period.

"The Midnight Snack," one of the "Five Old Favorites" group, depicts the adult Merrill going to the refrigerator at night, wrapped in apprehensiveness because of a lingering childhood memory of his father's flaring temper. "Childlessness" depicts his guilt at not continuing the family line and, thereby, frustrating his parents. It is one of Merrill's most exposed poems. The dream scenario centers initially on an archetypal garden where "Nothing is planted" (28). Later, the image of the sunset evokes not only the earlier theme of unrealized possibilities, but emphasizes the fact that time had run out: "A sky stained red, a world / Clad only in rags, threadbare" (29). The depth of Merrill's guilt is shown in the derisive image of himself as a "tiny monkey" who "puzzles over fruit" (28). The diminutiveness is an important aspect of the poem's reflection of the cultural myths reviewed in the poem: children are meant to have children; only then do they themselves escape being children. The final, grisly image of Merrill's parents being eaten to the "bone" by the stigma of his childlessness marks the experience in this poem as another firing point in his autobiographical drama. Throughout the 1960s he was to chart the awesome potency of the family in determining and defining the self.

"An Urban Convalescence" is an ambitiously long autobiographical poem, one of the watermarks of Merrill's career. The poem is a retrospective look at the years in New York before he moved to Stonington. "An Urban Convalescence" opens *Water Street,* just as "A Tenancy," which is about the house in Stonington, closes it. The speaker, after a week in bed, strolls along New York streets, feeling dislocated by the ceaseless demolition of buildings in his neighborhood. A sculptured stone garland remembered from the lintel of a demolished doorway reminds him of an inexpensive engraving of garlands in which he had wrapped flowers given to a woman in Paris whose face he cannot quite remember. The associative sequence is a convincing portrayal of the sifting of memory and the selectivity of consciousness.

The demolished surroundings also epitomize for the speaker his own sense of failed connections. In this context he finally perceives New York itself as a failure in his experience—a false start. Gradually, the confused images of New York and the rushing images from the past yield to a deeper and more constructive need, a "dull need to make some kind of house / Out of the life lived, out of the love spent" (6). The house is a central motif in Merrill's work, usually symbolizing the totality of one's experience. The spontaneous streaming of images that characterizes the first part of the poem thus gives way in time to the sense of a cohesive purpose beneath the randomness as the speaker, initially exposed and disoriented, turns into himself for warmth and comfort.

The poem's imagery is fundamentally surrealistic. Explorative perceptions compete with each other for authenticity within the speaker as he attempts to get his footing. The contending voices are given a musical structuring, as can be seen in the division of "An Urban Convalescence" into an introduction, a shrill, nervous allegro, and a final series of slow, tight quatrains that stabilize the dazed poem.

By way of contrast, "A Tenancy" deals with Merrill's settled life in Stonington, although there are flashbacks to an earlier tenancy after the war when he had rented a furnished room in New York. In spite of Merrill's balancing of the New York and Connecticut settings, the poem leans toward Stonington as the place of arrival. Stonington is also the focus for the theme of survival that threads its way through the poem. Reflecting on the distance he has travelled since renting the furnished room in New York, Merrill writes:

> The body that lived through that day
> And the sufficient love and relative peace
> Of those short years, is now not mine.
> Would it be called a soul? (52–53)

Bewildered by the metaphysical complexities of considering a succession of selves, Merrill escapes from the recesses of memory in order to welcome visitors bearing gifts who also arrive in March, stamping themselves "free of the spring's / Last snow":

And then, not asking why they come,
Invite the visitors to sit.
If I am host at last
It is of little more than my own past.
May others be at home in it. (53)

"A Tenancy" points up Merrill's growing sense of the psychic importance of setting. "I always find," he has confided, that "when I don't like a poem I'm writing, I don't look any more into the human components. I look more to the *setting*—a room, the objects in it. I think that objects are very subtle reflectors. When you are in an emotional state, whatever your eye lights on takes on something of the quality of a state of mind.'"[3] The power of setting can be felt in "After Greece," which illuminated Merrill's ambivalent feelings about America. Acknowledging the dominance of American culture in the contemporary world, he nevertheless felt himself longing for the "Essentials" of Greece: "salt, wine, olive, the light, the scream" (13).

"Roger Clay's Proposal" is unusual among the poems in *Water Street* and is probably as close as Merrill ever came to social commentary— with the possible exception of *Mirabell* (1978). Clay, an extension of the Charles persona, languidly proposes a ceremonial execution of world leaders as a solution to international tensions, "say in Rome or Nice— / Towns whose economy depends on crowds" (37). Both here and in "After Greece" Merrill shows a satirical intolerance for heated discussion of political and social issues and a corresponding faith in the power of ordinary realities—light, memory, ocean, love—to see man through. This, more than anything else, is what the poems in *Water Street* have in common.

Nights and Days

The excellence of the poems in *Nights and Days* (1966) was recognized when the book received the National Book Award in 1967. Although *Nights and Days* showed Merrill at the top of his form, the award was remarkable at a time when American poets were generally committed to eye-catching, socially relevant writing. The title of the collection, which is reflected in poems like "The Thousand and Second Night" and "Days of 1964," was drawn from the writings of the turn-of-the-century Greco-Egyptian poet Cavafy, whose focus on

everyday life and candor about homosexuality Merrill had decided to
emulate.

"Days of 1964," which is set in Athens, is an uninhibited celebration
of love. Indeed, the speaker risks the ironic hope that his love "would
climb when it needed to the heights / Even of degradation" (56).[4] The
poem skirts the evanescent boundaries of love, wavering between
ecstasy and a feared disillusionment: "A god breathed from my lips. / If
that was illusion, I wanted it to last long" (56). Eros is "masked" in the
poem not only by laughter and pain but by sexuality, causing the
speaker to question whether love transcends carnality. The ambiguity
of the poem's viewpoint is symbolized by Merrill's housekeeper, Kleo,
who is seen alternately as whore ("*Eat me, pay me*—the erotic mask /
Worn the world over by illusion") and as an aging woman faithfully
trudging over the pine-covered hillside to take care of Merrill's house in
Athens (55). The enigma of love, inextricably part of the "simple need"
of sexuality, became in *Nights and Days* a touchstone for Merrill's
dualistic expectations about man (55). Man is an animal driven by a
sexual hunger that masquerades as love; man is also, though, somehow
capable of genuine love.

"From the Cupola," which draws on the myth of Eros, is one of
Merrill's major poems. This long and complex work combines narrative, autobiographical, mythic, and lyric elements into one of Merrill's
densest and most elliptical poems. He described the genesis of "From
the Cupola" to Ashley Brown:

At first it was just a little poem in the first person. It was involved with a
curious experience—receiving letters from somebody I never met, who
seemed to know everything about me. I'm not paranoiac, but it was rather
unsettling. After a while I became engrossed with this interior experience. I
didn't want to meet the writers of the letters; I wanted to detach myself from
the experience to write about it. The poem from the beginning needed
"body" and I gave it this by way of landscape—what I can see from this
window. And then I thought of Psyche. Psyche, you know is a Hellenistic
myth. I also liked the "montage" of Hellenistic Alexandria and Stonington,
which likewise has a lighthouse and a library. Well, it *is* ambitious, but the
first and last parts, I think, tone it down—I frame it in "my own voice."[5]

"From the Cupola" intertwines three stories: the ancient myth of
Eros and Psyche, the contemporary version of that story involving

Merrill's "sister" and an anonymous admirer, and finally Merrill's own concealed story, "something I'm going to keep quiet about."[6] In the Greek myth Eros places Psyche in a dark place, warning her of dire consequences if she should ever see him. Overcome by curiosity, she does see him by lighting a lamp, and he flees. The myth underlines the traditional, allegorical role of Psyche as the soul, and thus points to the concealed theme of the poem—the speaker's love for his soul.

The relationship between Psyche and her brother ("James") is as important as her relationship with the anonymous admirer whose ardent letters so perplex her. Significantly, in terms of both the narrative and allegorical levels of the poem, the desire to know the identity of the mysterious letter writer is offset by a desire not to know: "Truth asks / Just this once to sleep with fiction, masks / Of tears and laughter on the moonstruck page" (38). To unmask Eros would risk disillusionment. Unlike the Psyche of the myth Merrill's heroine prefers the darkness. Through the sustaining of a highly charged atmosphere, which is reinforced by the heightened, often obscure speeches of the characters, Merrill wanted to create the illusion of a god's immanent presence. He regarded the motif of the stranger who knows one very well as "practically a metaphor for God," and echoed Borges's view that love is the founding of a religion "with a fallible god."[7]

Although the action of the poem, brief enough in itself, centers on the anxieties of Merrill's sister concerning her anonymous correspondent, the poem is rooted in the landscape of Stonington with its appropriate Greek architecture. There are two cupolas in the poem, the one in Stonington and the one that is the speaker's head. The anchoring of the poem in its gleaming, classical seaside setting is crucial to the design:

> Renaissance features grafted onto Greek
> Revival, glassed, hexagonal lookouts crown
> Some of the finest houses in this town.
> By day or night, cloud, sunbeam, lunatic streak,
> They alternately ravish and disown
> Earth, sky, and water. (39)

The freshness and concreteness of the setting reassure the reader's mind in its wanderings among the poem's elusive feelings whose meaning Merrill himself has said he does not fully grasp.[8]

Stonington's white pillars also prepare the reader for the encounter
with Eros:

> Our town is small
> its houses built like temples
> The rare stranger I let pass with lowered
> eyes   He also could be you. (39)

The figures in "Under the Cupola" conceal their realities from each
other (mask imagery is pervasive in the poem), just as the poem artfully
conceals its meaning from the reader; behind the masks, however, is the
desire to protect and nurture love. For this reason the speaker confides
to his mysterious soul at one point that the "mouths behind our faces
kiss" (40).

The centrality of the narrator's role is underlined in the middle
section, which focuses on Merrill's childhood years in Florida, a
flashback that is triggered by the "dwarf Palm" in Merrill's apartment.
Palm Beach had generated a sense of the ineffable in the young Merrill,
an effect that parallels the emotion generated by his sister's nameless
lover. Florida is presented as a timeless world "where nothing changed
or died / unless to be reborn on the next tide" (40). Merrill's youthful
Eden is a city that was "half desert and half dream." The sequence is
dominated by the memory of a royal palm that covered the young
Merrill's imagination with its shadow, that of a *towering mother / smooth
as stone and thousandbreasted*" (41). Recollection of the experience
prompts the adult Merrill to talk his sister out of her terror over her
anonymous correspondent, simultaneously allowing himself to grapple
with his own lingering fears. While using irony to tame subconscious
fears, he also talks lovingly in a hushed voice to Psyche—to his soul—in
one section of the poem: "She is more strange than Iceland bathed all
night / an invalid in sunshine Lava cliffs / The geyser that erupts the
loon that laughs" (43).

The Stonington cupola, whose circumference of glass symbolizes the
mind's multiple perception of reality, has its windows cleaned in the
poem. The wiping, however, simply sharpens the ambiguity of vision
by showing the self's mirrored involvement with everything it sees:

> Up here among
> spatterings and reflections wipe as I will

these six horizons still the rain's dry ghost
and my own features haunt the roofs the coast. (43–44)

The speaker's acceptance of these unresolvable complexities is rewarded
by a dream vision "unclipped by faith or reason" of angelic Eros (44).

In the fourth section Merrill subjects the theme of love to burlesque
treatment. Here, instead of the fertile, visionary darkness of dream,
there is the darkness of the merely literal. The scenario is that of a
drive-in movie under an evening rain. The speaker peers out at both the
screen and those parked nearby:

In the next car young Eros and his sweetheart sit
fire and saltwater still from their embrace
Grief plays upon his sated face
Her mask of tears does not exactly fit

The love goddess his mother overflows a screen
Sixty feet wide or seems to   Who can plumb
those motes of rose and platinum
At once they melt back into the machine. (48)

As in "Days of 1964," the speaker is baffled by the dualism of love,
which at times seems to be no more than lust and second-rate illusion.
Although Merrill was somewhat apprehensive about the effect of the
drive-in scene, aware that it might undercut the elevated mood of other
sections of the poem, he felt that it was as necessary as the poem's
physical surroundings, which also remind the reader of factual realities.

The final section of the poem opens on an early spring dawn which,
through the newly cleaned windows of the cupola, offers a clear, fresh
view of the Stonington waterfront. The speaker emerges out of his
reveries into the concrete autonomy of the external world. He focuses at
first on the literal scene, absorbed by a faded, red warehouse, but he also
foresees the "whitewinged boats" that will scud across the bay in the
summer light, an image that recalls the earlier visitation of the dream
angel (51). The moment captures the interplay of conscious and subconscious images and Merrill's acceptance of the plasticity and ambiguity
of vision. Recalling the play of light on the Palm Beach pavement that
had so aroused his youthful imagination, he now accepts the mingled
contraries of light and dark which, like the interfusion of the soul and
love, constitute the "dance I know / that cracks the pavement" (50).

Toward the end of the poem the image of the looming, royal palm is supplanted by harmless parsnips, which the speaker sets about gathering for his sisters, who have come to visit. Even here, though, he discovers that two of the parsnips have grown "tightly interlocked" like lovers (51). He buries them in "memory of us," he himself coming forward at this point as both Eros and Psyche (51). In preparation for the evening meal he and his sisters light the lamp, the interior lamp of the soul, which shines most brightly against the surrounding darkness.

Although the poem contains many obscurities, its delicacy of mood, undercurrent of tenderness, and visual unity allow its power to be felt. Consistent with the poem's themes, the language appeals to the ear and the subconscious rather than to the conscious mind. Through its combination of calculated reserve and spacious lyricism "Under the Cupola" epitomizes Merrill's fondness for buried meaning, his delaying of the mind's peremptory need to know by immersing it pleasurably in a strangeness it can be taught to trust.

The love poems in *Nights and Days,* such as "Between Us," are suffused with a happiness that runs throughout the poetry of the 1960s. Even in "The Thousand and Second Night," a long, discursive poem based in part on the *Arabian Nights,* vicissitude and despair yield eventually to a vision of love. The poem's contents are heterogeneous to say the least: the tale of Scheherazade, an attack of facial palsy, a visit to the Hagia Sophia in Istanbul, a visit to a Turkish bath, a bout of depression in Athens, a cache of pornographic postcards in an old photo album. The mixture of subjects preordained the slow emergence of the poem's structure from within, and also permitted Merrill to indulge his fondness for interruption and detour.

The title of the poem alludes to Scheherazade's survival of a sultan's cruelty through the art of storytelling. The poem in turn depicts Merrill's survival of the accumulated burden of his past through art and through love. "Rigor Vitae," the first section, recounts the effects of the awkward paralysis that froze the right side of his face in Istanbul. Taken aback, he decides to go sightseeing anyway on the first day of spring, beginning with a visit to the famous Hagia Sophia. The ancient structure, a church turned into a mosque, had in recent times thinned out to become merely a shell of its former, venerable self—a "flame- / less void" (4). Ironically, having vaguely hoped to escape introspection by entering the "transcendental" world of the Hagia, Merrill finds that he is thrown back upon himself by the resemblance between the denuded church and his own deteriorating life: "You'd let go / Learning and faith as well, you too had wrecked / Your precious sensibility" (5).

"*The Hamam*," the second part of the opening section, describes Merrill's visit to a Turkish bath. He goes there on the advice of a pharmacist, who recommends it for his paralyzed face. On the way to the bath, which is in the old quarter of Istanbul, Merrill is overtaken by a childhood memory. The prose jottings, which relay the immediacy of the memory, stand out against the surrounding quatrains of this section like a promise of movement amidst the stiffness of Merrill's face. The memory is about his grandmother's hand and ring. He compares his childhood view of his grandmother's hand to the "mosque of Suleiman the Magnificent, mass and minarets felt by someone fallen asleep on the deck of his moored caïque" (6). The shapes of Istanbul, mirrors of oriental mysticism, awaken a dreamlike stillness in Merrill which not only recalls pleasurable moments in childhood but also evokes images that are connected with his having become an artist. Looking through the straits of Bosporus toward Asia, he thinks of the

> "death-in-life and life-in-death" of Yeats'
> Byzantium; and, if so, by the same token,
> Alone in the sleepwalking scene, my flesh has woken
> And sailed for the fixed shore beyond the straits. (7)

Merrill's awakening to his vocation as an artist is linked ingeniously with the present, unreal paralysis of his face. The face becomes at this point a symbol of art, suspended between the empirical world and dream.

Section two, "The Cure," is set in Athens, where, although Merrill's face has been restored, part of him remains "cold and withdrawn" (7). He cannot shake a bout of accidia that drains his interest in the architectural beauty around him and saps his interest in others. In a park he puts off a Greek man who wants to make conversation, and later feels helplessly detached when he learns of the man's accidental death.

Section three, "Carnivals," sustains the poem's mood of alienation, and sends Merrill on a gloomy, retrospective search of his experience: "I wanted love, if love's the word / On the foxed spine of the long-mislaid book" (10). Looking for traces of past love, he finds only sexuality: "A

thousand and one nights! They were grotesque / Stripping the blubber
from my catch, I lit / The oil-soaked wick, then could not see by it"
(10). He therefore comes to perceive his present alienation as continuous
with a past that only superficially drew him into contact with others.
Section three touches bottom with "Postcards from Hamburg, Circa
1912." The pornographic postcards, found unexpectedly in an album
left by a recently deceased uncle, depict fellatio in a carnival setting.
The stanzas gradually flow away from the postcards into a series of prose
quotations that move the poem's center of gravity away from lust to the
general relationship between body and soul.

Imperceptibly, the language arrives at a vision of love against the
background of Merrill's leaving his Mediterranean surroundings for the
New World:

> Love. Warmth. Fist of sunlight at last
> Pounding emphatic on the gulf. High wails
> From your white ship: The heart prevails!
> Affirm it! Simple decency rides the blast!—
> Phrases that, quick to smell blood, lurk like sharks
> Within a style's transparent lights and darks. (12)

The tenuous affirmation of love is based upon Merrill's sense that his
"libertine" past did, after all, portray a man "in search of his soul" (12).
He tests this at once, however, by exhibiting a self-conscious wariness
about the language of love.

The setting changes to a carnival in the West Indies where a macabre
dancer in a "suit of bones" picks Merrill out of the crowd. The
bewildering sea of masks dissolves as he awakens in his bed in
Stonington. The section concludes with a grateful, redolent tribute:

> Lost friends, my long ago
> Voyages, I bless you for sore
> Limbs and mouth kissed, face bronzed and lined,
> An earth held up, a text not wholly undermined
> By fluent passages of metaphor. (14)

Merrill's "text" is that of his life, now accepted in memory and as part of
the art that, flowing out of it, is finally indistinguishable from it. The
poem thus arrives at that most elemental and indispensable of loves in
Merrill's writings, the love of self.

The desiccated mood of section four, a waggish mini-lecture on the preceding parts, comes as a shock. The section, though, is perfectly consistent with Merrill's dialectical method and outlook, his penchant for keeping everything in a state of taut, dynamic suspension. The fifth section is a vignette of Scheherazade on the night after her serial ordeal ended, the thousand and second night. The mood is quiet and dignified, the phrasing sonorous and rounded. The imagery continues the motif of the relationship between body and soul in blissful submission now to the mystery of experience, too "late to question what the tale had meant" (15). The tight versification formalizes the reconciliation of the opposites of soul and body, fact and dream, and seals the poem's experiences and memories in a shroud of language that will paradoxically protect them from decay. In the words of the mini-lecture in section four: "Form's what affirms" (15).

Although not nearly as strenuously as "The Thousand and Second Night," other poems in *Nights and Days* extend Merrill's autobiographical quest. "A Carpet Not Bought," for example, wittily opens up a whole new area of experience by focusing on things that have *not* been done. The poem describes an occasion renounced, an impulse mastered. The speaker, who has resisted the enticement to buy an expensive Persian rug, is tormented in sleep by a vision of the rug's beauty. On awakening he is filled, though, with a compensatory vision of the woven beauty of his own marriage.

Most of the poems in *Nights and Days* sound a note of affirmation. This note is especially audible in sunny poems like the "Little Fanfare for Felix MacGowan," which was dedicated to Merrill's grand-nephew. Even on less likely occasions, as in "Violent Pastoral," a tenacious mood of ecstasy overcomes the brutality of the predatory scene:

> Against a thunderhead's
> Blue marble, the eagle
> Mounts with the lamb in his clutch:
> Two wings, four hooves,
> One pulse, pounding, pounding. (19)

In a similar mood of affirmation Charles throws off the pain and duress caused him by a boor at a cocktail party with a panache and courage that constitute a victory of the spirit ("Charles on Fire," 25).

Occasions of defeat in *Nights and Days* are pressed into gold, as in "The Broken Home" in which Merrill looks back on his parents' divorce. His memory of his father's heady pursuit of wealth and wives, of his mother's desperation, and of his own Oedipal feelings coexists with his ironic recognition that he is still bound to his parents by an umbilicus of steel: "They are even so to be honored and obeyed" (29). The toy lead soldiers on the windowsill symbolize Merrill's passive isolation as a child bearing the brunt of his parents' separation. The image of the soldiers is associated with the emergence of a "heavy, silvery, pliable" feeling that prepares him stoically to face the rest of his life (29). While certainly not buoyant, the poem affirms the past by linking it through wry understatement with the survival of the cosmos: "Always that same old story—Father Time and Mother Earth, / A marriage on the rocks" (28). Similarly, the red coat of the Irish setter that Merrill makes part of the Oedipal scene in his mother's bedroom becomes centrifugally transferred to the image of the setting sun at the end of the poem.

The high energy level of *Nights and Days* is also reflected in the poems about music, one of Merrill's major interests. The poems "Balanchine's" and "Discothèque" are paired in an incisive musical contrast entitled "Watching the Dance." "Balanchine's," which is named after the famous Russian choreographer, describes the art of classical ballet whose supernal beauty, evoked by "unseen powers twirling on their toes," induces a belief in the fresh worlds that are created on the stage ("Observe the powers. Infer the stream" [36]). By way of contrast, in "Discothèque" Merrill produced one of the most devastating images of popular culture to be found in contemporary writing:

> Having survived entirely your own youth,
> Last of your generation, purple gloom
> Investing you, sit, Jonah, beyond speech,
> And let towards the brute volume VOOM whale mouth
> VAM pounding viscera VAM VOOM
> A teenage plankton luminously twitch. (36)

Echoes from Puccini's opera *Tosca* appear somewhat incongruously in "Maisie," which deals with the post-spaying depression of Merrill's cat. The effect is double-edged. On one level the operatic motif is simply mock-heroic, a way of reducing the emotion devoted to an animal. On another level, though, the music grandly enlarges the scale of the animal's existence. "The Mad Scene" originated in Merrill's memory of Joan Sutherland in *Lucia di Lammermoor.* After seeing the opera, he had a "dream called Laundry," which sprang from the picture of Sutherland, billowy and gory, moving across the stage. In the dream Merrill assumes feelings of heroic grandeur, circumventing the skepticism of his waking life. Both opera and dream transform him, permitting him to put on clothes of a "new fiber that never stains or wrinkles, never / Wears thin" (37). The image glows with an incandescence that is present in nearly all of the poems in *Nights and Days,* a collection that is a hallmark of Merrill's art.

The Fire Screen

The image of fire is everywhere in *The Fire Screen* (1969) giving the book a unity of effect that distinguishes it from preceding volumes. The image of the fire screen appears in "Mornings in a New House," which can be informally considered the book's title poem. The poem depicts a man awakening to find a blaze in the fireplace and the frozen windows thawing. The scene stays in his mind as, days later, he adjusts the screen in front of the fire. The screen is an old wood-framed one on which his mother as a girl of eight had made a crewel-work picture of *her* mother's house. Gradually, the speaker is drawn back in memory to his own origins, visualizing his mother as a child holding a doll that was destined to become himself. He identifies with the held doll, imagining his mother having "sung to him, let him fall, / Howled when his face chipped like a plate" (40). [9] His mother exists in his mind as a "tiny needlewoman," an image that not only captures her childhood, but links her with the woven house on the fire screen (41). She is miniaturized both by the distance of the past and by the surrogate world of art.

Merrill intensifies the poem's effect by introducing through a footnote the motif of the screen of fire that protects Brunhilde in Wagner's *Nibelungen* cycle. Awkwardly intrusive in some respects, the footnote evokes connotations that are latent in the imagery even if it brings in others that appear extraneous. Through the Wagnerian reference the fire screen thus comes to symbolize not only the membrane of memory but also that of passion:

He stands there wondering until red
Infraradiance, wave on wave,
So enters each plume-petal's crazy weave,
Each worsted brick of the homestead,

That once more, deep indoors, blood's drawn,
The tiny needlewoman cries,
And to some faintest creaking shut of eyes
His pleasure and the doll's are one. (41)

Merrill's passionate links to his mother and to his childhood generate a
wave of feeling that reaches deep into his adult life (symbolized by the
"New House" of the poem's title) with feelings that are both painful
("blood's drawn") and reassuringly pleasurable.

"Mornings in a New House" is typical of many of the poems in *The
Fire Screen* in that it opens vividly with a sharply defined scene and then
moves on through memory to a reawakening of past emotion that
ultimately brings discovery. "A Fever," which deals with another form
of fire, opens with the speaker in bed and in a delirium. The virus had
been given to him by a female visitor who returns at the end of the
poem. The action involves a hallucinatory encounter between the
speaker and a doll on his dresser who is embittered at having been
abandoned. Passing out of the fever, the speaker awakens to greet his
returning visitor, savoring the "thin paints" of her lipstick upon his
tongue and thereby establishing a link between her and the doll whose
lips, he had noticed earlier, his own lips had "effaced" (39, 37). As in
"Mornings in a New House," the doll becomes a childhood prototype
for the shape of later emotion in spite of Merrill's skeptical disclaimers
in the poem: "Asleep in a chest you kept informed on the middle-aged /
Me who loves Verdi and Venice, who registers voters?" (38).

The screen of memory also dominates "The Friend of the Fourth
Decade." Hearing that a friend renews his life periodically by removing
the stamps from old postcards through soaking them and erasing their
messages, the speaker decides to give it a try. He finds, however, that
the erasing process does not work, and he becomes absorbed in the
forgotten correspondence. The poem's couplets illustrate the two-
sidedness of the speaker's debate with himself, and it becomes gradually
clear that the "friend" of the poem's title is actually an alter ego. On the
one side is the speaker's intimate attachment to the past in spite of an
accompanying sense of loss. On the other hand, he longs to escape the

ennui of being imprisoned in a life and time he knows too well, and imagines a future wherein his consciousness and memory are stripped in order that he may make a fresh start:

> Behind a door marked DANGER
> (This is a dream I have about my friend)
>
> Swaddlings of his whole civilization,
> Prayers, accounts, long priceless scroll,
>
> Whip, hawk, prow, queen, down to some last
> Lost comedy, all that fine writing
>
> Rigid with rains and suns,
> Are being gingerly unwound. (8)

The unwrapped figure, who resembles the blank postcards the speaker's "friend" successfully unfurls, emerges at the end of the poem as the "perfect stranger," an entirely new self for the reflexive self to explore (9). The appearance of the "perfect stranger" wistfully symbolizes the wish for a release from relentless introspection—a momentary desire to fly from the self. The image is also a foreshadowing of Merrill's later attraction to the myth of reincarnation.

"The Summer People," a long narrative poem, offers a mellower view of memory. The poem is a ballad about life in Stonington, specifically about four of Merrill's friends, the four in fact to whom *Water Street* is dedicated. The four characters in the poem are Margaret, her daughter Nora, Andrew, and his wife, Jane. They are joined in time by a newcomer to town, Jack Frost, who, although he symbolizes winter and aging, becomes the lively center for a time of the little group of summer residents.

The summer people play bridge together, party together, do everything together for a number of years, snugly insulated from the year-round residents of their community who include a large group of Portuguese immigrants. Jack, appropriately ageless-looking to suit his semi-allegorical role, stays through the long winters, and draws the others to give up their seasonal flights to tropical climes. Thus do they gracefully enter the aging process, feeling initially invigorated and renewed by the experience. The relationships sour in time, though, and Jack leaves the community for good following an altercation with Margaret after his cat bites her.

With Jack's departure (he leaves Ken, his tipsy Japanese servant, behind to mind the house), the other four lapse into an apathetic routine, having clearly lost their taste for life:

> Languid as convalescents,
> Dreading the color green,
> They braced themselves for summer's
> Inexorable routine. (68)

As it happens, the four summer people miss the meeting where a chemical plant is permitted to enter the town, a plant that eventually destroys the beauty that attracted them to the town in the first place. The poem slopes inexorably toward its conclusion. The suicidal death of Ken finishes the cycle. The summer people sell out and disperse, not before hearing Jack's long silent piano played, though, by a Portuguese grocer's son, now a student at the Massachusetts Institute of Technology. He inherits a world whose style and grace they carelessly let slip away.

While the poem's ballad stanzas mock-heroically contrast with the distinctly antiheroic aloofness of the summer people, something of the pathos and gravity of the ballad tradition enters at the end in Merrill's final view of the town:

> One window framed the sunset
> Transfiguring Main Street,
> Its houses faintly crimson
> But upright in defeat. (76)

Having taken his leave of the town, Andrew, like one of E. A. Robinson's bleak figures, "shut both views behind him / And felt his way down in dark" (77).

The parade of monosyllabic words and masculine rhymes tends to stiffen Merrill's portrait of the characters and their situations, draining them of subtlety if not of irony. He gives them a form whose robustness simplifies their drama and its meaning. The poem is thus a *form* of memory, one way of remembering things, set against other, quite different and usually more searching ways in *The Fire Screen*. The firmness and simplicity of Merrill's approach in "The Summer People" produces a bright hard appearance that makes everything in the poem look boldly vivid. Jack's renovation of the old Baptist Church is an example:

> The church was now a folly
> Cloud-white and palest blue—
> Lanterns, stained glass, mirrors,
> Polar bear rugs, bamboo,
> Armchairs of gleaming buffalo-horn,
> The titter of wind chimes,
> A white cat, a blue cushion
> Stitched with the cat's name, Grimes. (59)

The poem's urbanity, precision, and lightness of texture remind one of Pope—with whom Merrill later connects himself in "The Book of Ephraim." Also reminiscent of neoclassical art are the ironic juxtapositions and witty transpositions:

> Andrew at the piano
> Let the ice in his nightcap melt.
> Mendelssohn's augmentations
> Were very deeply felt. (57)

The poem's lively style and the underlying sympathy of Merrill's viewpoint inject vitality and warmth into a tale that otherwise documents the bleak effacing of time and the heavy cost of ignorance.

As "The Summer People" demonstrates, memory in these poems is a fire screen that entices the voyaging mind toward the glowing core of past experience. In "Matinees" Merrill recalls being brought by an adult friend to a Saturday afternoon performance of the Metropolitan Opera in New York. The experience revolutionizes his life and sets him on the path of art. Dropped into a sea of adults, he nonetheless responds eagerly to the haunting, Wagnerian strains and to the magic of the stage, which had become a "rippling azure scrim" (47). Recognizing his dentist in one of the roles, he quickly forgets actual life as he sinks beneath the spectacle and music, discovering the fiery aspirations of his own soul as the heroine flings "Kisses into the furnace roaring praise" (49). Poems like "Pola Diva" and "The Opera Company" explore the emotionally volatile world of opera singers. In "The Opera Company" the rival sopranos wage a long and stormy campaign against each other:

"The maid of one was sent / To fumigate the prima donna's dressing room / After the other had used it" (44). Again, as with the allusion to the dentist in "Matinees," Merrill polarizes the mundane lives of the women (one was reported to have opened a "ranch for divorcées") and their equally authentic, heroic presence on stage. If life often divides, the poem suggests, art reconciles. This is symbolized when Merrill listens to the two sopranos singing duets on an old recording, the cover of which shows them smiling and with "linked arms" (45). The antagonism between the singers has receded into the past ("One is old now, one dead"), but their voices "soar and mix" and "will not be told apart" in the speaker's "spinning heart" (45).

In addition to memory, art in "The Opera Company" is portrayed as a screen of fire which is tacitly put in place by both artist and audience, each standing on one side of the screen—the artist ready to create the illusion, the audience ready to suspend disbelief. The unspoken pact between artist and audience hovers over those entering the stage door of the opera house:

> Prompter, electrician, negro star,
> In street clothes, disappear
> Through the unmarked stage door, rust-wreathed and massive.
> *Addio,* one or two will say, *leb' wohl,*
> And press my hand as if I, not they, were leaving.
> *Look for us. We have chosen*—no—*You chose* . . .
> (The point will be to close
> With their exact words—only by luck, however,
> Reconstructable in dim suspense
> Before the curtains part.) (46)

The allusion to the "negro star" symbolizes the social changes that have occurred at the Met since Merrill's youth. Continuing beneath these changes, however, are the timeless ground rules of art, the mutual agreement between performer and audience to temporarily exchange a mundane, "street clothes" world for a magical one.

Lovers in Merrill also place a similar sort of fire screen between themselves, one whose transforming power continues as long as the lovers will it. Typically, the poems depict the cyclical progress of the illusion. Characteristically, the lovers fear that their assent to the illusion is not reciprocated, and this forms the basis of poems like "Part of the Vigil." In that poem Merrill constructs an elaborate conceit in which the speaker wanders through the chambers of his lover's heart seeking evidence that an ikon of himself is present there. He emerges from his journey without finding such evidence, but is reassured that, whatever the lover's heart contains, his own heart, as yet unpoisoned by jealousy and suspicion, continues to love: "Didn't your image, / Still unharmed, deep in my own saved skin / Blaze on?" (25).

"Flying from Byzantium," which describes a separation, interlaces the motifs of love and art. The poem describes a departure from the Byzantine part of the world which Merrill inhabited for part of the year. The "priceless metal bird" melds the images of modern jetliner and Yeatsian golden bird (31). The flight symbolizes the transitory ecstasy of love and art amid convincing, mundane realities. Merrill makes it clear that even a defunct love continues to burn in the artist's vision, if nowhere else. Thus, the end of the affair in "Flying from Byzantium" involves a final view of one of the lovers as a "young scribe," who having "turned a fresh / Page, hesitated," and "dipped his pen" (31).

Greece was another fire screen for Merrill. Never doubting his essential difference from the Greeks he lived among, he was nonetheless attracted by the fiery Greek temperament in spite of its moral ambiguities: "scheming, deluded, gifted, noble, weak."[10] Above all, as can be seen in "Another August," he loved the Greek sun and the simplicity of his Athenian house near its pine-covered hillside:

> Pines. The white, ochre-pocked houses. Sky unflawed. Upon
> so much former strangeness a calm settles, glaze of custom to
> be neither shattered nor shattered by. Home. Home at last. . .
>
> Here is each evening's lesson. First
> the hour, the setting. Only then
> the human being, his white shirtsleeve
> chalked among treetrunks, round a waist,
> or lifted in an entrance. Look for him.
> Be him. (35)

Increasingly in the 1960s Merrill felt the development of a Greek self, and he came to feel warmly at home with that self even if the barrier of language was always present. His difficulties in mastering the Greek language can be seen in the humorous poem "To My Greek." Amid the strenuous social debates in America during the 1960s, however, he turned with relief to his homely Greek, which was limited to a concrete, practical vocabulary for the most part: "Let there be no word / For justice, grief, convention" (19).

His portraits of Greek friends focus on their habits of speech, as in "Kostas Tympakianakis" and "Words for Maria." With a single utterance he often creates a rounded sense of a character's presence, as in Maria's raucous *franglais*: "Eh, Jimmy, qui sont ces deux strange men?" (12) Maria Mitsotaki (née Demertzís, 1907–1974) was one of Merrill's closest friends, and became one of those recurring figures in his poetry whom the reader comes to know so well. In spite of his somewhat derisive portrait of her as a talced actress in an uproarious comedy of manners, he loved her "Sweet good nature" and "lack of guile," which he regarded as symbolic of the healthy openness of Greece (12). Merrill and Jackson met Maria in Athens in 1962. She was the daughter of a former Greek prime minister and the widow of a well-to-do Greek businessman who had died shortly after the Second World War. The marriage had not been a happy one. Like Merrill, she had travelled extensively in the 1950s. She was not a literary person; Merrill portrays her in the poems as earthy and lively though not especially gregarious. Indeed, one cannot help but sense both the lonely depths of her independence and the compensating warmth of her attachment to Merrill. The depth of *his* attachment to her can be seen in his later assigning of the role of Beatrice to her in his divine comedies.

"David's Night in Veliès" describes a night spent by David Jackson in a farmhouse while traveling in the mountains of the Greek Peloponnesus. The poem depicts the way in which Greece refreshed the senses and imaginations of both Merrill and Jackson. Jackson is served a "Cyclopean" meal by an epic "Godmother" who smokes the food by "Lulling the olive boughs" (33). The hearth scene, another of the book's magnetic images of fire, has such a forceful effect on Jackson that he feels the moment's lustrous memorableness even before it slips into the past. He tries to cram the sensations connected with his visit to the farm into a present ecstatic moment before dropping off to sleep, including the foreseeing of his departure in the morning:

> The road would climb in bracelets toward the pass,
> The sun be high but low,
> Each olive tree shed its white thawing shadow
> On sallow grass,

> Myself become the stranger who remembers
> Fire, cold, a smile, a smell,
> One tiny plucked form on the embers,
> Slow claw raised in blessing or farewell. (34)

The final images of the fireplace and of the small bird, which the farmer had gone out to shoot for Jackson's breakfast, idyllically consummate the experience. The poem, set in modest quatrains, is one of Merrill's finest.

The mood of fullness that characterizes many poems in *The Fire Screen* swells with the recollection of the many things Merrill had received from time. The mood is offset, however, even though in a minor key, by a note of ebb and dismay. Merrill reminds himself, for example, of what life would be like without love in a poem about the shark and its familiar parasite:

> Pea-brained, myopic, often brutal,
> When chosen they have no defense—
> A sucking sore there on the belly's pewter—
> And where two go could be one's finer sense. ("Remora," 36)

A few of the poems dwell on the relationship between man and animal, a relationship that also involves a dividing screen of sorts. Man and ape are related in "An Abdication," which, in anticipation of the later divine comedies, places the relationship against the larger canvas of evolution:

> My cousin's eye
> Lights on a rust-red, featherweight
> Crown of thoughts. He seems to wait
> For me to lift it from my brow (as I
> Now do) and place it smartly on his own. (26)

"The Envoys," three exquisite poems about animals—a scurrying lizard, a scarab beetle, and a kitten—are timeless, emblematic pieces reminiscent of Merrill's earlier work. A few of the poems exhibit a new interest in the unfolding of history, anticipating *Braving the Elements*. Among these are "An Abdication," which has already been mentioned, and "Lorelei." "Lorelei" is based on the legend of the siren who lured sailors to their deaths on the rocks of the Rhine. Without softening the impact of the legend, Merrill depicts the rocks as stepping-stones as well as gravestones, ways to the future based upon the accumulated wisdom of those who have gone before. He portrays the sequence of history on an intensely personal as well as on a collective level, gathering all of the poem's figures under the metaphor of stranding. The image ambiguously combines the idea of being stranded and the picture of bits of strand or beach, the one a symbol of defeat, the other of fortuitous survival. The bald couplets and condensed symbols of "Lorelei" give the poem an almost runic force. Merrill was gradually moving away from a focus on the slender filaments of personal history to the larger patterns of anthropological time. While *The Fire Screen* cannot be described as a transitional volume, it does represent a peak of sorts for the Proustian poems of recollection that began with *The Country of a Thousand Years of Peace.* The very ripeness of Merrill's handling of these themes, then, was a signal to the watchful reader that some sort of change might be expected.

Braving the Elements

Braving the Elements (1972), which was awarded the Bollingen Prize for poetry, reflects Merrill's shift away from personal autobiography to the autobiography of the planet. The book contains a number of long poems that reveal an ambitious structuring and an increasing complexity and density in phrasing. In a sense, the collection can be seen as a culminating one since the elements of fire and water, for example, had already figured in the titles of previous collections of poetry. Nevertheless, Merrill turned toward nature with unprecedented interest in *Braving the Elements,* particularly in the poems which grew out of his visit to the Southwest. A number of the poems have outdoor settings and show an intense awareness of the earth's geological past.

All the same, Merrill was aware of the irony of picturing himself as braving the elements: "Elizabeth Bishop, when I told her the title, remembered an old lady she used to visit in Maine who on a windless July day would take a walk with her companion, wrapped up in scarves and coats, and someone looked out of a window and said: There is Miss So-and-So braving the elements, which is pretty much the way I thought of the title, too."[11] The title of the book comes from the poem "Dreams about Clothes" in which Merrill somewhat skeptically questions the influence of art on life:

> Won't you help us brave the elements
> Once more, of terror, anger, love?
> Seeing there's no end to wear and tear
> Upon the lawless heart,
> Won't you as well forgive
> Whoever settles for the immaterial?
> Don't you care how we live? (61–62)[12]

Here, the elements are psychological ("terror, anger, love") and even art is of limited use in dealing with them. The poem strikes a note of resignation that is characteristic of *Braving the Elements,* which has attrition as its principal theme.

The attrition of the heart is portrayed in "Flèche D'or," which is named after the European passenger train that carries the speaker away from an extinguished love affair. The train's name, the "golden arrow," refers explicitly to the myth of Eros and the defenselessness of those who are struck down by love. The cycle of love, so overwhelming in both its coming and going, is linked to the continuum of time, which like the parallel tracks, appears to offer no break in the cycle. Alluding implicitly to the Greek philosopher, Zeno, who argued that a moving body never came to the end of a line, the speaker longs for some omnipotent cosmic observer "in whose heart of / Hearts the parallels / Meet and nothing lasts and nothing ends" (63).

The austere mood of *Braving the Elements* is particularly apparent in the poems about the Southwest. In these poems Merrill often places the affective qualities of human relationships against an immense non-human world. "Nine Sleep Valley" is a sequence of nine poems connected loosely by setting and theme, one for each of the nine days spent by two male lovers vacationing in the Southwest. The title creates a montage in which the lovers' nights merge with the sleeping eons of geologic time that surround them. In the first poem, a Shakespearean sonnet, the speaker announces his intention to interpret his surroundings, to "read in Nature's book / The pages" (30). All he gets, though, is a fleeting impression of his environment ("canyon forest landslide lake"), finding that nature's "words have wings" (30). Bewildered by the multiplicity of nature's forms, he flounders until the natural objects around him are given meaning by his companion who, "Fluent and native," interprets them (30). The second poem, composed of three quatrains, is a flashback that depicts the speaker's exit from the city to visit the Southwest. The startling allusions to the assassinations of

Robert Kennedy and Martin Luther King drive the image of urban culture into the poem like a wedge, allowing the reader to experience the speaker's relief in leaving society behind in order to enter the world of nature. The third poem, a single haiku stanza, wipes out the threatening images of social turmoil in a blissful view of the lovers at dawn.

In the fourth poem the lovers set out on a hike in the heat of the day. The sky is a "high pool deep blue very hot / Illumination of the brimstone text," a smelting fire that purgatorially hovers over the aridity of the sandstone canyons around them (31). The way of the poem is up—into the heart of the cosmos: "Ice in the marrow of a star so pure / So beyond history" (31). The fifth poem, a sonnet in couplets, shows the hikers coming upon a long abandoned prospector's cabin in some trees along a river. At this point mythic images of American history enter the poem:

> Look. Out of thin air old gods (plume, hide, bead)
> Appear to weigh your offerings of seed.
>
> A leathery prospector god's pans fill
> With foolsgold facets of my blackbird's trill. (32)

Merrill evocatively interfuses the white man's past—including treacherous dealings with the Indians in the nineteenth-century scramble for gold—with the present treasures of the scene, the aspen's "seed" and the "blackbird's trill."

Poem six elaborates the motif of the prospector's cabin, which is now portrayed as a "flask" containing a past that the two hikers have "uncorked" so that "two rooms / Are won back to this world" (33). The hikers try to recreate the lives of the prospectors to the "last friend's guitar and stories" and finally down to the last, lonely prospector who is swallowed up by modern America. The past includes the lovers' present experience, which will eventually be someone else's past and which will inevitably invite a paradisal reading from those looking back at it: "*Here all would have been well*" (33).

The seventh poem, written in ballad-like quatrains that end in the same, rhyming sound, involves a ghostly meeting between a dead person and a speaker who ponders the past. Each perceives the radiance of the other, each convinced of the reality of a day, never his own, when "beauty, death, and love" are "coiled together in one crowning glory" (34). The central motif of the eighth poem is a geode, a nodule of stone containing a cavity lined with crystals or mineral matter. It is here that Merrill unites the beauty of his human lovers with that of their eroded surroundings. Geodes, when cracked open, reveal rich, interior waves of color that contrast with their drab, crusty exteriors ("Rind of crystals velvet smoke meat blue"), having been formed, like the lovers,

> under fantastic
> Pressures, then cloven in two
> By the taciturn rock shop man, twins now forever
>
> Will they hunger for each other
> When one goes north and one goes east? (34)

The geodic cavity evolves into a symbol for all of nature, including man: "Centimeters deep yawns the abyss" (34).

The final poem, which is composed of three quatrains, sums up the major themes of "Nine Sleep Valley" with its pronounced, unifying rhymes of "heart," "dark," and "art" (35). Nature is "dark" in that it ultimately resists man's efforts to encompass it through understanding. It has also been darkened by man, who has disfigured its ecology just as he has marred his own history—as the earlier allusions to political assassinations and Indian massacres indicate:

> Master of the ruined watercolor,
> Citizen no less of the botched country
> Where shots attain the eagle, and the grizzly
> Dies for pressing people to his heart,
> Truster, like me. (35)

In shooting the eagle, America has symbolically taken the final step toward its self-destruction. While Merrill's allusions to topical events in "Nine Sleep Valley" disturbed those readers who felt that they endangered the poem's integrity, the allusions indirectly imbue the image of nature with great value. Furthermore, through the symbol of the geode—and indeed through the lovers themselves—Merrill implies that paradise is still accessible within the world of the present.

"In Monument Valley," which is set amid towering, sandstone monoliths on the Arizona/Utah border, is a study in both personal and ecological attrition. The arid foreground with its wandering, starved horse—still "half in trust, half in fear of man"—is juxtaposed with an earlier, idyllic summer evening in upper New York state when Merrill rode horseback in the soft light of dusk:

> Stillnesses were swarming inward from the evening star
> Or outward from the buoyant sorrel mare
> Who moved as if not displeased by the weight upon her.
> Meadows received us, heady with unseen lilac.
> Brief, polyphonic lives abounded everywhere. (10)

While Merrill is outwardly a survivor in comparison with the "stunted, cinder-eyed" horse that approaches him as he sits in his air-conditioned car, he is nevertheless moved to consider his own aging as he drives away from the doomed horse, which is now too weak even to eat (10). Acute, tactile contrasts give the poem a well-honed vividness.

The elements themselves speak in "The Black Mesa" and "Banks of a Stream Where Creatures Bathe." The black mesa, addressing the low flatland around it, recaptures for a moment some of the grandeur of its past. The "viceroy's eagle" recalls the Spanish presence in the Southwest while the "turquoise" is a reminder of the native, Indian culture of the area (42). Both enrich the value of the mesa, which, all the same, will continue to erode until, as Merrill puts it in a final pun, "all be plain" (42).

"Under Libra: Weights and Measures" is one of the more opaque poems in *Braving the Elements*. In a letter Merrill has sketched the background of the poem, which he described as "scenes of semi-rural life outside Santa Fe":

I was staying with a friend who rented a house near the church and graveyard—probably I stole something of the Chimayo graveyard, too—on a ranch full of peacocks. From Santa Fe you can see the Los Alamos lights at night; a friend called them the "necklace of death." Angel Ortiz is simply the type of an old Spanish-American settler. Blanca is a dog, the Gem is a razor blade, the Swan is the constellation, though I'm also thinking of those swans of ice which cradle caviar at fancy receptions. The house where I visited had on a wall a huge white blanket woven with a black two-headed bird.[13]

The allusion to Libra places the time of the poem as mid-fall, but the opening refers to the "stones of spring," just one of many examples of balance that echo the astrological significance of the title. The poem begins with a description of some ancient stones that have been introduced into the speaker's house, where they are used as paper-weights and doorstops. In spite of the pragmatic uses to which the stones are put, their effect is to remind the speaker of the vast scale of geologic time that dwarfs his own scale of living. The effect of this reminder, however, is unexpectedly positive since he "learns / To live whole days in another / Tense, avoid the bathroom scales or merely / Sing them" (44). The speaker passes from the world of the mundane ("bathroom scales") to another *scale* of things entirely, a scale in which movement is measured by the "riverbend's great horseshoe print" (44). The panorama of the New Mexican terrain dramatizes not only the wide sweep of geological time but also the cyclical return of ecological history upon itself. In this way it neatly meshes with the motif of the seasons that circulates through the poem. The associated image of the sun moving across the sky balances Santa Fe with its eastern counter-part, Stonington, the place from which Merrill had set out. Time and again images of personal significance—such as the lichen-covered stones that are souvenirs of Merrill's trip to the Southwest—are bal-anced against parallel images in the natural world, like the giant boulders left by receding, ice-age glaciers "Dragged south in crushing folds, / Long dirty tablecloth of ice" (43).

"Under Libra" is an elaborate, symbolistic collage of imagination, space, and time containing strands of burnt landscape, anthropological dream, and actualized nightmare (Los Alamos's "necklace of death"). On a deeper level Merrill was working toward the sort of unifying, cosmological synthesis that was to emerge in the divine comedies. Here, already, he portrays minerals flowing into plants ("Copper, silver, green / Engraved by summer's light, by spring's") which in turn flow into a relativistic matrix of space-time (44). The poem is dazzl-ingly modernist in both thought and execution.

The dual focus on attrition and on the massive backdrop of the inorganic in *Braving the Elements* underlines the transitoriness of life, as is seen in the image of the flame in "Log": "Dear light along the way to nothingness" (3). Large chunks of history flash by with each click of a string of Greek worry beads in "Komboloi." Similarly, Merrill con-structs a huge historical circuit in "Pieces of History" that joins the ancient Egyptians and the American astronauts. In "Mandala" the self spins toward extinction along with the rest of the universe, resisted only by the spiral of reincarnation, which has its own disadvantages:

One wants, to plot the boomerang curve
That brings one back,

Beyond the proper coordinates of Have and Lack,
A flair for when to swerve
Off into utter pointlessness— (22)

The stoical mood of these poems is epitomized in the compass rose
image at the end of "Syrinx":

                          Nought
                Waste   Eased
                          Sought

Ostensibly in a state of balance between negative and positive forces,
the universe, with its human passenger, slopes inexorably toward
disintegration with love only sporadically holding back the "great god
Pain" (72–73).

The somberness of *Braving the Elements* hangs over the autobiographical reminiscences as well. In spite of the winsome qualities of
"Days of 1935," Merrill's concluding tribute in the poem to the
"golden haze" of his past is deliberately hackneyed and bitter: "Those
were the days" (21). The poem is based upon a contrast between his
actual childhood in the 1930s and a fantasized, compensatory version
which he invented as a child in order to cover his growing loneliness.
The young Merrill lies awake in his room at night while his parents are
out partying, and his nurse, who was "old and deaf and slow," is off in
the servants' wing listening to the radio (11). Having been provoked by
accounts of the Lindbergh kidnapping, he imagines himself in a
semiconscious dream to have been abducted by a pair of kidnappers,
Floyd and Jean. They whisk him off to their hideaway, a "hovel in the
treeless / Trembling middle of nowhere" (11).

The poem's strength lies in its projection of the combined viewpoint
of the emotionally charged child and the retrospective urbanity of the
older Merrill. Both views converge in the description of Jean:

              A lady out of *Silver Screen*
              Her careful rosebud chewing gum,
              Seems to expect us, lets us in,
              Nods her platinum
              Spit curls deadpan. (12)

The passage's erotic overtones, which reflect Merrill's candor in describing his nine-year-old self, are also implicit in the description of Floyd:

> The man's face
> Rivets me, a lightning bolt.
> Lean, sallow, lantern-jawed, he lays
> Pistol and cartridge belt
> Between us on the oilskin (I
> Will relive some things he did
> Until I die, until I die). (12)

Sexual connotations surface more explicitly as Floyd sleeps beside the child:

> Small fingers felt,
> Sore point of all that wiry meat,
> A nipple's tender fault.
> Time stopped, His arm somnambulist
> Had circled me, warm, salt as blood. (19)

Together with the child's witnessing of the sexual play of his kidnappers, their "prone tango," the surrounding erotic language reveals the fantasy as in part a liberation from the conventional inhibitions of his upbringing (15). Hollywood B-films and movie magazines, which serve as the model for the amorous adventures of Floyd and Jean, evidently provided the young Merrill with the taste of forbidden fruit:

> And one night—pure "Belshazzar's Feast"
> When the slave-girl is found out—
> She cowered, face a white blaze ("Beast!")
> From his royal clout. (15)

The kidnappers gradually assume a more poignant role in the fantasy as surrogate parents—as can be felt in the scene in which Jean watches as the child drops off to sleep: "I felt her watching from her chair / As no one ever had" (13). The kidnappers became alternate models by which the child can assess his actual parents, whom he imagines receiving the ransom note:

> My mother gloved,
> Hatted, bepearled, chin deep in fur.

Dad glowering—was it true he loved
Others beside her? (14)

The final scenes of the dream, which depict the capture of Floyd and
Jean, point not only to the child's guilty feelings about choosing new
parents for himself, but show as well how even dreams become infil-
trated by a stubborn, underlying sense of reality. The beginning of the
end comes when Jean reveals her ingenuous sense of reality:

"Do you know any stories, Kid?
Real stories—but not real, I mean.
Not just dumb things people did . . ."
I stared at her—*she* was the child! (16)

At this point the roles reverse, and the child becomes the storytelling
parent to the kidnappers, which both fits his actual role as the creator of
the fantasy in which they appear and which also silhouettes his loneliness. The depth of that loneliness is revealed in the way in which by
inventing and telling the story to himself he becomes the parent he
never had. As in "From the Cupola" the self would have to comfort the
self.

Following the dream, Merrill returns to the actual world in a scene in
which the child, parentless for all practical purposes, watches the cook
baking. Later, his father sips a bourbon in the den while leafing through
the *Wall Street Journal,* and his mother quickly kisses him good night
before greeting another influx of guests:

Tel & Tel executives,
Heads of Cellophane or Tin,
With their animated wives
Are due on the 6:10. (21)

The biting puns of the quatrain underline the complex tone and mood
of the poem which resist nostalgia even while evoking it in a struggle
against the glib tendency of memory to sweeten and embellish the past.

"Up and Down" comprises two poems in a subtle, antithetical
relationship to one another. "Snow King Chair Lift," the *up* poem, is a
euphoric recollection of a ride up the mountain by two lovers who gaze
their "little fills at boundlessness" (55). The ride, which symbolizes the
love affair, takes them to a summit that is a "cul-de-sac" from which

there is nowhere to go but down. The poem thus contains a modest counter movement to the prevailing mood of uplift. Similarly, in "The Emerald," the *down* poem, there is a countervailing resistance to the mood of declivity. The poem describes Merrill's visit to his mother after the death of her second husband. Together, they go down into the vault where she keeps her valuables. There, she offers her son an emerald ring that had been given her by his father when he was born, suggesting that he keep it for his future wife. He declines and slips the ring on her finger.

The poem's burgeoning ironies include the name of the bank ("Mutual Trust") and the fact that Merrill survives the deaths of his mother's two husbands to—metaphorically, at any rate—become the third. The Oedipal fire of earlier poems gives way here, though, to a simple acceptance of what it is too late to alter: *"We are each other's; there will be no wife; / The little feet that patter here are metrical"* (57). The *"green room"* of the emerald whose light envelops both Merrill and his mother is the room of art as well as the room of age. The emerald image combines both the morbid connotations of the "vault" and those of the offsetting, heightened chamber of art, both the inertness of the hard gem and the hope symbolized in its visionary green. Hence the slight upturn at the end: "The world beneath the world is brightening" (57).

"18 West 11th Street" is the address of the New York house where Merrill spent part of his childhood, a house which was blown up in 1971 by the left-wing group the Weathermen, who had been using it as a temporary headquarters for making bombs. One of the group's members was Cathy Wilkerson, daughter of the vacationing financier who owned the house. Some of the Weathermen were killed when a bomb accidentally exploded, and the girl was seen by witnesses running from the building, naked and bleeding. She vanished into hiding.

Merrill compares his own uneventful growing up with that of the equally affluent but revolutionary girl who succeeded him in the house. He perceives the suffocating limitations of his background, limitations that in retrospect seem to merge with the decor of the house:

> Item: the carpet.
> Identical bouquets on black, rose-dusted
> Face in fifty funeral parlors,
> Scentless and shaven, wall-to-wall
> Extravagance without variety. (25)

Merrill's deepest instinct, however, is to conserve and to bridge the
generational gap, as his own writings attest. It is in this respect that he
most forcefully distinguishes himself from the Weathermen:

> In what at least
> Seemed anger the Aquarians in the basement
> Had been perfecting a device
>
> For making sense to us
> If only briefly and on pain
> Of incommunication ever after. (24)

The Edenic illusions of the Weathermen, which when punctured lead
to vindictive violence, are mirrored in the name pronounced by Cathy
Wilkerson on fleeing the burning house: "She stirs, she moans the
name / Adam. And is *gone*" (28).

The poem does much to explain Merrill's disaffection with the
1960s. If he resented the insensitive rapacity of his parents' generation,
he was outraged at the hypocrisy of activists who in the name of justice
reduced to rubble what offended them and who appeared to live in a
haze of mind-numbing slogans—"Rebellion . . . Pentagon . . . Black
Studies" (24). The poem is noteworthy for its admixture of blunt,
colloquial, angry speech and the language of elegant disdain. Also
memorable is the juxtaposition of the stark scenes of urban blight—the
smoking ruins, the police floodlights, the lingering pools on the
street—and the faint, lyrical echoes of a lost childhood.

"Days of 1971," which consists of a series of alternating Italian and
Shakespearean sonnets, recounts an automobile trip taken by Merrill
and his Greek friend, Strato, through France, Italy, and Greece. Strato,
with whom Merrill had been involved sexually for some years, is
another of those recurring figures in the poetry. The poem's sarcastic
tone sets clear limits on the relationship, which had become stale over
the years. In spite of this, the mood lightens as they stop to visit old
friends, and encounter some ravishing sights, particularly in Venice,
where through its "vertiginous pastry / Maze we scurry through like
mice" (67). The image of Venice finally deepens the mood of decay,
however, and Merrill ponders the erosive effects of the sea on the
baroque city, which is described as "Crumbling in the gleam of slimy
knives" (67). The poem later touches bottom in a scene in which a

landslide forces Merrill to interrupt his journey and to line up for
overcrowded ferries: "One self-righteous truck / Knocked the shit out
of a eucalyptus / Whose whitewashed trunk lay twitching brokenly"
(68). As in "18 West 11th Street," the language is unusually bold and
raw.

The poem lifts at the end, though, as Merrill unwraps a delicate
figurine which Strato had given him after visiting the famous glass-
making area of Murano near Venice:

> Two ounces of white heat
> Twirled and tweezered into shape,
> Ecco! another fanciful
> Little horse, still blushing, set to cool. (69)

The token rescues the fading affair for another day, though on the
whole the poem underscores Merrill's preoccupation in *Braving the
Elements* with attrition. "Strato in Plaster" sets this theme in a humorous light with a contrast between the aging Strato in a plaster cast and
the image of his earlier firm attractiveness. The submerged motif of the
plaster cast as a forerunner to a finished marble enters the poem through
the image of the Apollo statue. The statue recalls the physical beauty
that Strato once had as well as symbolizing the permanence of art as
opposed to the transience of life and love.

The book's atmosphere of sinking aftermath is nowhere more visible
than in the title of "After the Fire," a poem that refers directly to the
imagery of *The Fire Screen* and by implication to the vitality of Merrill's
earlier poems. Rooms in Merrill's house in Athens had been repainted a
"quiet sensible light gray" after a fire that occurred in his absence (5).
The new sober coloring effaces the past look of the rooms and therefore
to some extent the past itself including its scenes of love. Kleo, Merrill's
longtime housekeeper, visits him with a cake, complaining, though,
about her mother's senile rages, her daughter's looseness, and her
brother's sordid homosexual adventures. Merrill visits Kleo at her
house, and seeing that the brother has taken over some of his pos-
sessions, theorizes that he might also have set the fire. At this point all
of Merrill's past relationships in Greece appear to sink into a melancholy
gloom. Suddenly, though, the grandmother, a "little leaden oven-rosy
witch" (5), returns to sanity and recognizes her guest: *"It's Tzimi! He's
returned!"* And with this recognition, the speaker notes, she was

restored to "human form" (7). The change alters the mood of the poem from sullenness and betrayal to dignity and a gratitude for the past as Merrill kneels before the old woman "pressed to her old burning frame" (7).

Amid the images of decay and fiery destruction in *Braving the Elements* are faint signs of renewal—as in "Yam": "Rind and resurrection, hell and seed, / Fire-folia, hotbeds of a casserole / Divinely humble" (41). The apotheosis of the humble vegetable points to a rallying energy that will in time drive the divine comedies. Paralleling the oppressiveness of loss and betrayal is the mind's fecundity, which can people the heavens and earth, though not quite as quickly or triumphantly, as decay and reversal can unpeople them.

The Yellow Pages

Published in 1974, *The Yellow Pages* contains poems written from 1947 to 1972. A photoduplicated version of the collection, entitled *59 Poems,* slightly different from the final printing, had been run off in 1971. The poems were those that, for one reason or another, Merrill found unsuitable for earlier volumes—hence, the motif of *yellowed* pages. He thought of *The Yellow Pages* as an offering to friends, and felt that it should not be given the status of a new book of poems.[14]

Stretching out over such a long period, the poems are as diverse in quality as they are in subject. Early poems like "The Diary of the Duc de L*** have little in common with more recent works like "Child of the Earth" and "Desert Motel with Frog Amulet," which resemble many of the poems in *Braving the Elements*. A few of the poems, like "Europa" and "From *The Broken Home*," are prototypes for later poems. There are travel poems, emblem poems, a Dorothy Parker monologue ("642719"), and a Charles poem ("Table Talk"). There are tributes to Vermeer ("Delft"), Albert Camus ("Autumn Elegy") and William Carlos Williams ("Opaque Morning"). There are brimming epigrams, like "Cupid," which was written in the mid-1960s, and fine satiric vignettes, like "Lunch With a Scholar," which was written in the early 1970s. Some of the poems, like "Music from Above" (1960) and "Landscape with Torrent" (1958) are ineffectual, and probably should have been left in the drawer. Most, though, deserve to have seen the light of day even if on the whole they do not represent Merrill's strongest work.

Perhaps the most distinctive poems are the concise, still-life sketches with their surprising subjects, "Landscape with VW" (1969) being a good example. The noisy little Volkswagen, with its homely insect body, becomes a "votive spansule" which carries its weary passenger off into the countryside to "cub and violet, your whole wildlife / Sanctuary hurt into blossom, healed by it" (30). [15] The sketches frequently hinge on puns and proverbs—as in "A Silence" (1968): "No coffin without nails. / This one you drive into mine / At least is golden" (51). The little love poem offers a tissue-thin section of an experience whose delicate transparency reveals unexpected depths.

"Opaque Morning" (1963), which was written on the death of William Carlos Williams, is equally satisfying visually. On this occasion Merrill adopted a spare, imagistic style which resembles that espoused by Williams. The opening view of the sky, "Cold mottles gray," in particular recalls Williams's famous poem "By the Road to the Contagious Hospital" (63). Merrill takes the occasion to affirm the resilience and power of art against mortality: "We strain to see beyond the stone / That has soaked upward into words / That have soaked downward into it" (63). The interlacing of the words of the dead poet and those on his gravestone illustrate the theme that, if death ultimately shapes the artist, art in turn shapes life and in this respect at least protects it from decay.

A similar affirmation is found in "Delft" (1961). Vermeer is depicted as having painted the drowsy town so definitively that the speaker finds it impossible to perceive the actual town without his own view being overshadowed by the Dutch painter's impression of it:

> Houses left to steep
> In teabrown water
> Stretch and totter
> On the brink of sleep. (47)

"Early Settlers" (1958) anticipated Merrill's poems about the Southwest, and although it yields to fancy, its portrait of the pioneer couple who are defeated and then assimilated by the elements, is unforgettable: "Gnarled, then ashen, upon some hearth not seen / But tended in impassive silence by / A leathery god or two, crouched there for warmth" (14). "Child of the Earth" (1969), about a non-poisonous scorpion found drowned in a friend's pool, is one of Merrill's best poems about the Southwest. Attracted to the pool area at night by "small

purple / Windfall plums," the animal falls into a "great crystal reliquary / Between the desert and those nodding / Trees of heaven, as
they call them here" (72). In its "sheepskull visor" and "shiny brown
armor" the creature, it occurs to Merrill, is no less nor more "plausible"
looking than the man and poodle looking down at it.

The theme of the earth as the mother of all life takes on visionary
significance in "Desert Motel with Frog Amulet" (1969). The visionary
impulse combines with the green amulet so that for a moment the
desert surroundings are miraculously liquefied: "Deep in the waste one
room was green as water / And tall erosions rippled what it faced" (70).
While the visits to the deserts of the Southwest developed Merrill's
anthropological consciousness, it was the visionary practices of the
Indians that most absorbed him. As early as 1959 in "Words for the
Familiar Spirit" he rose to a vision of the sacred quetzal of the Mayans.
In parallel fashion, in poems like "The Case Worker" (1965), an
indictment of bureaucratic welfarism, he focused on the impotency of a
visionless America awash in its own advanced technology. Nevertheless, skeptical about the transcendental overtones of visionary art, he
held off until the mid-1970s when, stimulated by the open-ended time
schemes of geology and anthropology, he realized that the scale of a
single human life, which had always been his measure, was vaster than
he had at first imagined.

Chapter Six

The Divine Comedies

Beginning of the Trilogy

"The Book of Ephraim," a startling ninety-page, spiritualistic poem that was included in *Divine Comedies* (1976), marked the opening of a new phase in Merrill's writing. *Divine Comedies,* which was awarded the Pulitzer Prize, also contains some autobiographical poems that show Merrill at the top of his form. Merrill intended the poems, which exhibit a complex weaving of narrative and lyrical elements, to lead up to the epic "Book of Ephraim," the first part of his trilogy of divine comedies. The prefatory character of the shorter poems can be seen in "The Kimono" with its allusion to reincarnation, a motif that is central to "The Book of Ephraim": "Desires ungratified/ Persist from one life to the next" (3). In addition, the poem's polarities—fire and ice, white and blue, water and plant, winter and summer—evoke a dialectical image of the flow of time that is also consistent with "Ephraim."

"McKane's Falls," which was set in the Southwest, also considers the Heraclitean flow of time, here symbolized by the rushing of water. The scene begins with two nineteenth-century prospectors searching for gold in a high mountain stream. Their effect on the stream traumatically increases the ecological rate of change since they alter the shape of the stream bed in digging for gold. Their activity is seen as a prelude to the massive changes that man would bring to rivers in the twentieth century, particularly through hydroelectric power developments that would turn pellucid mountain steams into silty, murky basins. The elements of permanence in the poem appear to be mostly sinister. The acquisitive exploitation of the stream by the prospectors is paralleled by that of the power utilities; similarly, the enmity between the prospectors is paralleled by quarrels between the speaker and his friend while visiting the prospectors' old campsite. The poem reaches toward a point of reconciliation, though, in the perception that the two friends, while different from each other, have led complementary lives, lives of action and contemplation: "You played your part in a Far Eastern theatre. / I stayed home with Balzac, and meditated" (13). Together, the men make up a single, full life. The symbol for the reconciliation of opposites is the waterfall. Behind the world of mutability symbolized by streaming water lies a "chamber of black stone" that stands for the underlying stability of experience (13).

"Yánnina," which is set in the Greek town that served as the headquarters for the notorious Ali Pasha, also deals with the wheel of time, as in fact do all of the poems in *Divine Comedies*. Ali's history is recalled in tacky souvenirs sold along the Yánnina lakefront as well as in somber views of the island that was his final refuge before the Turks shot him to death. Also recalled is Byron's brief visit to Ali, including the despot's lascivious attempt to seduce the young Englishman. Merrill concentrates, though, on Ali's relationship to two women, "Frossini," whose chaste rebuff of Ali led to his ordering of her death by drowning, and "Vassiliki," the concubine who acquiesced and survived.

Throughout the poem the reader is made aware of resemblances between the gruff yet charming despotism of Ali and the manner of Merrill's own father. For Merrill the problems of interpreting political history were only slightly different from those of biographical history: "Historical figures are always so well lighted. Even if one never gets to the truth about them, their contradictions, even their crimes, are so expressive. They're like figures in a novel read by millions of people at once. What's terrifying is that they're human as well, and therefore no more reliable than you or I. They have their blind 'genetic' side, just like my boys and girls in Yánnina."[1]

He focuses on contemporary myths surrounding the two women in Ali's life. Like the woman in "Yánnina" who is sawed in two in the magician's tent, Frossini and Vassiliki seemed to Merrill to be two halves of an archetypal, female reality—a revered, virgin modesty on the one hand and a sinful, enticing carnality on the other. Merrill complicates the pattern by showing that Frossini's martyrdom has been reproduced on cheap postcards sold in kiosks along the waterfront, her "eyeballs white as mothballs, trussed / Beneath the bulging moon of Ali's lust" (25–26). The melodramatic pictograph of Frossini's story is juxtaposed with an unexpectedly dignified rendering of Vassiliki, thereby reversing the moral symmetry of the historical model. Merrill accomplishes the metamorphosis by placing Frossini and Vassiliki in a restricted, aesthetic perspective so that the reader judges them for qualities other than those of virtue. He does the same with the tarnished, historical image of Ali, bringing out his charm and the "whimsically / Meek brow, its motives all ab ulteriori, / The flower-blue gaze twining to choke proportion" (28). The poem suggests that the multiple, shifting perspectives of time and vantage point, while interesting in their variety, frustrate the mind's desire for order and meaning. Ironically, art with its avowed subjectivity, not history, can provide order and meaning, as is implied when Merrill sits down to write: "The lights wink out along the lake. / Weeks later, in this study gone opaque, / They are relit. See through me. See me through" (29).

"Lost in Translation" considers the relationship between memory and random experience. The foreground story concerns a rare and challenging, wooden jigsaw puzzle which Merrill's absentee parents sent to him as a child to help him pass the summer. He works on the puzzle with "Mademoiselle," the sympathetic governess who appears in other Merrill poems. Many of the puzzle pieces have interesting, definable shapes, one of which is that of a tiny palm tree. Merrill recalls the palm tree and the episode involving the wooden puzzle as, in the poem's present time, he puzzles over the whereabouts of his copy of Rilke's translation of Valéry's poem "Palme." The search opens up a knot of associations through his memory's resourceful tracking of analogous experience. On one level the poem is a paradigm of the mechanical tendency of memory to be stimulated and programmed by random signals. On another level, however, Merrill carefully illuminates the resemblances in experience that have enriched and delineated his life. In this way, the lines of Valéry's poem become relevant to his autobiographical reveries. Valéry describes the palm tree, for example, as seeking water beneath the desert, an analogy for the action of memory in Merrill's poem.

The process of memory is portrayed as one of translation, as the principal motifs suggest—Merrill's translation of Rilke, Rilke's translation of Valéry, the bilingualism of "Mademoiselle," the translation of the puzzle pieces into an intelligible order. Memory picks up the pieces of the past and places them into the full context of the mind's experience, just as the remembered figure of the sheik in the wooden puzzle comes to merge in Merrill's consciousness with the image of his father. Similarly, the Arabian scene which emerges when the puzzle has been completed contains the isolated figure of an attendant page boy who is mistaken at first for a "son"[7]. The incident becomes a melancholy reminder of the unfulfilled relationship between Merrill and his father. For a while the feet of the page boy cannot be found, but the piece is later discovered under the table. The feet symbolize the role of memory itself, which provides Merrill with images of childhood on which to place the adult edifice of his life. In this sense, memory is a kind of surrogate parent. Just as the governess took the place of Merrill's actual parents, so too the mind turns the apparent "waste" of experience into "shade and fiber, milk and memory" (10). In this way the random aspects of experience become the found order of a human life.

The motif of childhood is given heightened treatment in "Verse for Urania" and "Chimes for Yahya," just as that of old age is represented by the snowy, apocalyptic image of the Maharishi, father of transcendental meditation, in "Whitebeard on Videotape." "Chimes for Yahya," like "Lost in Translation," is as much about the act of remembering as it is about the memories recovered. The poem, a Christmas oratorio dedicated to a dead Iranian friend, opens in Athens on Christmas Eve. Greek children mill through the streets ringing Christmas chimes, whose sound at first irritates Merrill—though he soon adjusts. The experience unlocks a hoard of memories, beginning with a train trip to Florida in the company of his governess. His parents motor to Florida to better conceal from him the presents they are bringing for Christmas. His governess, however, had already allowed him to peek at his presents before the trip began so that that Christmas had a feeling of *déjà vu* for Merrill which, as is seen in his reaction to the chimes, "has been a problem ever since" (16).

A subsequent memory in the poem recalls Merrill's journey as a young man to the Persian capital of Isfahan to visit a "friend of friends" (16). Yahya, a young Iranian tribal chief who is later killed in a duel captivates Merrill's imagination: "Lover, warrior, invalid and sage, / Amused unenvious of one another, / Meet in your face" (18). Around Yahya are an old family retainer, Hussein, and a visiting, female, American anthropologist who is studying Yahya's people. As befits a Nativity story, Merrill's poem comes to center on a birth, that of one of the women of Yahya's tribe. The anthropologist, anxious to witness the birth and its ancient rituals, pressures Yahya into letting her be present. Caught off guard by his own ritual of mideastern hospitality, he gives in—even though this is a violation of his people's code of conduct.

Merrill and the anthropologist, "Staring like solemn oxen from a stall," witness the shadowy pageant of the birth, which is accompanied by appropriate moans from a "veiled figure writhing on a carpet." The scene erupts into comedy when light is applied and the mother is discovered to have been the old servant, Hussein, substituting for the real mother. While the incident satirically pinpoints the coarseness of the American anthropologist—and by extension that of her aggressive culture—its deeper function is to illuminate the superior insight, tact, and protectiveness of Yahya. Merrill's elegiac recollection of Yahya's charm, delicacy, and warmth forms the poem's emotional center, and becomes the basis for his revitalized appreciation of Christmas. Indeed, the thrust of the remembered emotion is powerful enough to reach even further into the symbolism of Christmas to a vision of a reunion with Yahya beyond this life where "friends arrange to be reborn together" (19).

Using a similar motif, "Verse from Urania" deals with the christening of a Greek-American girl who is given the name of Urania. The name, which means the "heavenly one," is shared by the Greek Muse of Astronomy and by the most recently discovered planet in the earth's solar system. Merrill, the child's godfather, lives in the apartment above Urania. The poem centers superficially on the cultural distance separating Greece and America, but the substantive contrast in the poem is that between the ancient world, which created astronomical myths, and the contemporary management of the heavens by a visionless technology. The present age, that in which the child will grow up, is visualized as one in which a "mill turned to maelstrom, and IBM / Wrenched from Pythagoras his diadem" (32). The image of the mill is an allusion to the influential study of mythology *Hamlet's Mill,* by Giorgio de Santillana and Hertha von Dechend, which Merrill refers to in an introductory note to *Divine Comedies.* Like these authors, he laments the contemporary demythologizing of Western culture that put an end to a long, mythic heritage wherein the "wealth of pre-Olympian / Amber washed up on the shores of Grimm" (32).

Staring at the night sky, Merrill feels an atavistic closeness to early man based upon the awakening of his sensibility at the sight of the stars:

> Adamant nights in which our wisest apes
> Met on a cracked mud terrace not yet Ur
> And with presumption more than amateur
> Stared the random starlight into shapes.

Millenia their insight had to flee
Outward before the shaft it had become
Shot back through the planetarium
Cathodic with sidereality. (33)

The image of delayed light finally arriving from outer space is in one
sense an acknowledgment that this is an age of science, but it also
symbolizes the recognition that ancient man's mythic charting of the
heavens was a projection of a genuine human glory.

In this way, Merrill, like the unbaptized child, is a "pagan," who
welcomes the christening as a time-honored ritual of renewal (31). Thus
is his paradoxical bond with the child "sacred, being secular" (36).
Moreover, Merrill's brand of secularism is viewed as far less harmful
than that of the materialism that has overtaken contemporary man
(including Urania's parents), a "twilight of the worldly goods," as he
puts it (35). The christening thus brings about the rebirth of the
godfather as well as the child, allowing him to enter a "second childhood" (35). In this renewed state he revisits not only his own but the
childhood of man, wherein he hears the primitive sounds of the "loud
dance, its goat-eyed leader steadied / By the bull-shouldered next in
line" (35).

As in "Chimes for Yahya" the poem is grounded in the Nativity
motif. That motif is represented in "Verse for Urania" by Purcell's
sacred song, the "Blessed Virgin's Expostulation," which Merrill listens to during the night in a room above those occupied by his new
godchild and her family. The song's simplicity and tenderness heighten
its rendering of a universal myth: "A schoolgirl's flight to Egypt, sore
afraid, / Clasping the infant, thorn against her breast" (36). Completing the poem's patterns of unity and renewal, the first rays of the
morning light touch Merrill's and Urania's apartments "Flooding both
levels with the same sunrise" (36). The poem, which unfolds simultaneously on personal, symbolic, and intellectual levels, is one of
Merrill's most flawlessly structured and deeply affecting works.

"The Will" is directly connected with events in "The Book of
Ephraim." The poem tells of Merrill's loss of the incomplete manuscript of a novel in an Atlanta taxicab. He had come to visit his mother
and had included with his luggage a carved stone ibis and the un-
finished novel. He had purchased the ibis, an ancient Egyptian symbol
of resurrection, with money his father had given him shortly before his

death. Among other things, the novel was to have been about a familiar spirit named Ephraim, whom Merrill and David Jackson had contacted during experiments with a Ouija board (a copyrighted device for the transmission of messages from the spirit world). Ephraim bears a striking physical resemblance to Meno, the attractive visitor who had appeared to Francis in *The Seraglio.* In addition, action at the Ouija board was to have been complemented by a Gothic story set in New Mexico involving characters who are described in "The Book of Ephraim."

The poem is organized around the motifs of will or legacy, sacred ibis, airplane, and the "burden" on Merrill of his father's death (39). The symbol of the carved ibis is all-encompassing, being used alternately with the "I" of the opening dreamscape as a symbol of art and as an emblem of life beyond death. Buoyed up by his spiritual alliance with the bird, Merrill moves back into the "weird / Basalt passage of last winter," a period that contains the secrets of the lost novel (42). The image of a lighted match evolves into a dim passage through the tomb of an ancient pharoah, a motif that through its focus on death and immortality blends with the metaphor of the ibis. The scene is a symbolic prelude to the novel's rebirth in the poetic form of "The Book of Ephraim." In parallel fashion, Merrill's spirits rise again with the plane that carries him home, his unsettled feelings of separation from his past finally overcome in a soaring moment in which a "healing hieroglyph" is cut out of the sky's blue "bone" (43).

"The Book of Ephraim"

A central aspect of the structure of "The Book of Ephraim," the major poem in *Divine Comedies,* is that of *pentimento,* the visibility of an artist's original and different idea beneath the surface of a completed painting. The lost manuscript of the New Mexico novel mentioned in "The Will," for example, lies visible beneath the varnished surface of "The Book of Ephraim." Merrill's original hopes for the novel are included in the important, prefatory section of "The Book of Ephraim":

> Fed
> Up so long and variously by
> Our age's fancy narrative concoctions,
> I yearned for the kind of unseasoned telling found

> In legends, fairy tales, a tone licked clean
> Over the centuries by mild old tongues. (47)

Merrill wanted characters who were "conventional stock figures /
Afflicted to a minimal degree / With personality and past experience"
(48). Appropriately, then, his cast included a "witch, a hermit, inno-
cent young lovers, / The kinds of being we recall from Grimm, / Jung,
Verdi, and the commedia dell' arte" (48). His intentions for the novel
carried over into "The Book of Ephraim" in that some of his novelistic
characters infiltrate the poem. Indeed, all of the characters in the
trilogy, suspended as they are in the occult, contribute to the fable-like
atmosphere that he had sought in the novel with their sudden appearances and unexpected pronouncements.

Among the characters from the novel who figure in the poem,
Joanna—the "witch"—is the most radical and unsettling. In Section J
of "Ephraim," she is pictured sitting in a plane with "Smoke pouring
from her nostrils" (77). On the poem's literal level, she is simply boozy
and volatile, but Merrill uses her to achieve the sort of Gothic ambience
that he wanted for the *Inferno* level of his divine comedies, which are
loosely patterned after Dante. Section J is named after both Joanna and
*J*ung, suggesting a third, psychoanalytic level in the poem that is
intermediate between the literal and the Gothically supernatural:
"Jung on the destructive / Anima would one day help me breathe / The
smoke of her eternal cigarette" (79). Joanna and Sergei, the poles of
good and evil in the uncompleted novel, were also "Vital to the psychic
current's flow" (79). For Merrill the contemporary, scientific expulsion
of good and evil starved the psyche, and "The Book of Ephraim" was
designed to nourish the collective imagination of the pragmatic,
"myth-starved" culture around him.[2] Appropriately, Rosamund
Smith, who is named as a character in the projected novel in "Ephraim," becomes "Mrs. Myth" in *Mirabell,* the second part of the
trilogy.

Merrill's decision to use material from Ouija-board conversations
involving himself, David Jackson, and the familiar spirit Ephraim
finally led him to the poem rather than the novel as the appropriate
genre. He felt the poem would be a less restrictive medium for such
unusual experiences. Furthermore, he had felt, even in the forty or fifty
pages of the missing novel, that he had dwelt too much on visual detail

and not enough on action, which he saw the novel as demanding. He had no idea on setting out that the accumulated poem would eventually run to three volumes and over 500 pages—even though at the conclusion of "The Book of Ephraim" the narrative situation is left hanging. On the other hand, the epigraph from the *Paradiso* that comes at the beginning of "Ephraim" is evidence that Merrill was open to the idea of a tiered poem like Dante's. While Merrill may not have seen beyond the end of "Ephraim" when he finished that work, it is evident that at the conclusion of *Mirabell* he clearly foresaw a third volume.

"The Book of Ephraim" involves an exploration of culture and mythology while *Mirabell* concerns itself with science and culture and *Scripts for the Pageant* is visionary. While comparable to modern poetic epics like *The Waste Land* in some respects, Merrill's bizarre spiritualistic format and camp humor distinguish "The Book of Ephraim" from the oracular gravity of Eliot's poem. On the other hand, the cosmological scale of "Ephraim," together with its sweep of intellectual history and formidable mythmaking root the poem in the epic tradition.

The myth announced for "The Book of Ephraim" is the "incarnation and withdrawal of / A god" (47), a phrase that Merrill drew from Northrop Frye's *Anatomy of Criticism* (1957). The myth is that of reincarnation and was originally to have centered around Eros, the name originally chosen for Ephraim in the lost novel. In the trilogy Ephraim symbolizes not only love in general but the particular love shared by Merrill and David Jackson since the 1950s. The Hebrew name Ephraim means *doubly* fertile. "The Book of Ephraim" traces the course of the love between Merrill and Jackson from its happy inception to its fading and its near extinction. Under the umbrella of the poem's prevailing myth of reincarnation, however, even the fading of that love, which is palpably felt at the end of the poem, can be seen as a prefiguring of its return.

In addition to being an incarnation of love, Ephraim has a narrative role in his own right. He is a first-century Greek Jew who was killed by the Roman guard under Tiberius's orders for having been the emperor's nephew, Caligula's, lover. On the principle of like being attracted to like, he was drawn to Merrill's and Jackson's Ouija board in 1955. As the willowware cup used as a pointer moved back and forth over the board for the next twenty years, Ephraim let his listeners in on the secrets of the universe—as *he* understood them. As a cosmic spokesman

on the bottom level of Merrill's trilogy, Ephraim's views are both
revelatory and limited. Similarly, the kind of love he symbolizes is
primarily sensual rather than elevated and spiritual.

The Ouija board itself became the basis for the structure of Merrill's
divine comedies. The letters of the alphabet, which are present on the
board, are the basic structural principle of "The Book of Ephraim."
Similarly, the arabic numerals on the board were to form the divisions of
Mirabell, and the words "yes" and "no" along with the ampersand sign,
which are also part of the Ouija board, would become the titles of the
three main sections of *Scripts for the Pageant.* The use of the alphabet as
the organizing principle in "Ephraim" connects that part of the trilogy
with language. As with the operation of memory in "Lost in Translation" the arrangement appears arbitrary, but this failed to prove a
handicap in the case of a responsive and vital inner order of experience
such as Merrill's life constituted.

Merrill has described his poetic transcriptions from Ephraim and
from the other familiar spirits in the trilogy as "pretty much verbatim"
even though carefully edited to fit into the overall design.[3] While
conceding that the communications from beyond, which were spelled
out letter by letter, might ultimately be projections from his subconscious, he insists on the authenticity of his extraordinary experience in
receiving these communications. In the case of "Ephraim" the messages
from the dead take up less space than Merrill's own words, whereas in
Mirabell the opposite is true, and the weary reader is faced by acres of
the uppercase type used to represent the voices of the dead. One among
the trilogy's many paradoxes is the fact that such a prolific series of
poems resulted from a growing number of deaths among Merrill's and
Jackson's families and acquaintances. In addition, as Dante had done,
Merrill relies in part on those he had loved to guide him through the
heavens, and, as in Dante, the journey is an ascending one.

"The Book of Ephraim" opens in Merrill's domed, red-walled
dining-room in Stonington with its milk-white oval table at which he
and Jackson have spent many evenings at the Ouija board. References
to the outside world are rather perfunctory compared to Merrill's other
work, particularly in the first half of the poem in which Ephraim makes
most of his appearances and in which Merrill and Jackson are at peace
with one another. The eclipsing of the external world symbolizes the

inwardness of the experience mirrored in the poem. One important external event recorded in the first half of the poem, however, is the death of Merrill's father, which occurs while Merrill is far from home. While the death affects the poet, it fails on the whole to compete with his subseqent excitement at the Ouija board. In fact the death is simply absorbed into the system of reincarnation that according to Ephraim governs the universe. Another digression that is skillfully integrated into the whole is Merrill's visit to a ranch in Oklahoma where chimpanzees are studied for human traits (Section F). The chimpanzees illustrate the cycle of reincarnation within the framework of evolution. One of the chimps, with the heavenly name of Miranda, kisses Merrill. The incident strengthens his growing belief in the unity of life even while, ironically, the unity of his own life with David Jackson is clearly waning.

Ephraim outlines a universe of nine stages—somewhat like Dante's—in which he himself is at stage six. The stages reflect a hierarchy of responsibilities and aptitudes within a system governed by disembodied patrons and their earthly representatives. The system is designed to provide lives that are as useful to the life process as possible. Merrill learns that his patron is a nineteenth-century editor of Alexander Pope, a revelation that he accepts as significant in the light of his own poetic practice. Promotion within the cosmic hierarchy ordinarily comes about when a representative with a reincarnated soul grows in wisdom to the extent that at death he is able to replace his patron, who in turn moves up the ladder. As in any bureaucracy, this one is subject to exceptions, though, so that Merrill's departed friend Maya Deren, the avant-garde filmmaker, for example, enters heaven directly, soaring above those on lower levels. Throughout "The Book of Ephraim" there is an eerie sense of higher powers who might and do intervene at any moment to regulate communications from the dead.

Outlandish as it is in some respects, the system allegorically underlines Merrill's belief in man's potentiality for cultural and spiritual evolution. More important, perhaps, the cosmic staircase of reincarnation described by Ephraim registers the triumph of the lingering human spirit against the amputating power of time. In terms of those of Merrill's dead friends who play a part in the trilogy, *their* spirits survive by lingering in the minds of those who survive them. In this way they work posthumously on subsequent generations through the memories of individuals and through the collective memory of civilization of which "The Book of Ephraim" is a part.

Underlying the organizational efficiency of the poem's reincarnational superstructure is Merrill's suspicion that all life forms are under the microscope of some unfathomable final will and intelligence— "subjects in a vast / Investigation whose objective cast, / Far from denying temperament, indeed / Flung it like caution to the winds, like seed" (63). This perception is part of the trilogy's pendulous motion between a belief that the future of all life depends critically on what man chooses to do and the equally credible belief that a vision and purpose clearer and stronger than man's will decide things.

Merrill's habitual skepticism about ideas forms an important aspect of "The Book of Ephraim"'s tone. His addiction to the Ouija board in the first half of "Ephraim," for example, together with his reiterated doubts about the revelations obtained at that board, paint an engaging and complex portrait of the whole mind—the venturing, impressionable part of the mind interlocked with its own built-in censor. Ephraim's unsentimental view of history also sets the tone for some of the poem's unnerving revelations. Mentioning that George Bernard Shaw in the afterlife had the unenviable task of taking charge of the soul of a newly dead boy who had been tortured and burned to death, Ephraim at first appears callous—"A FINE BROTH OF A BOY COOKED OVER FLAME"—but then adds: "I AM NOT LAUGHING   I WILL SIMPLY NOT SHED TEARS" (61). Merrill's urbane tone in "Ephraim" curbs the emotional effect of some of the atrocities recounted and stems the grief that could easily arise from thinking about the deaths in particular of those who had been close to him.

The most haunting atrocity mentioned in the poem is that of Hiroshima. The souls of those killed at Hiroshima are said to have been so annihilated by radiation as not to be reusable within the cycle of reincarnation. Hiroshima is thus not only a symbol of obliteration of all life but a reminder that in "The Book of Ephraim" soul and matter are coextensive terms. The dependence of soul on matter is symbolized on the narrative level by the fact that the world of familiar spirits is dependent on this world for its very existence. Ephraim, also, is portrayed as depending for his existence on the sustained love of Merrill and Jackson for each other. Apart from the threat of nuclear war, the other looming cosmic problem outlined in "Ephraim" is that of over-population, a peril that throws Merrill's guilt about childlessness in earlier poems into a new light.

Merrill's focus on the problems of nuclear warfare and overpopulation appears incongruous alongside the geniality and sumptuousness of the poem. The mind's ability to play in the face of danger, however, is for Merrill a sign of its glory and a reason to struggle for its survival. Thus, the imagery of doom is juxtaposed with passages that are airy in texture and feeling, as in the description of the inquisitive spirits who hover around the Ouija board: "Once stroked, once fed by us, stray souls maneuver / Round the teacup for a chance to glide / (As DJ yawns, quick!) to the warmth inside" (66). The description recalls Pope's depiction of the sylphs in *The Rape of the Lock.*

The turning point in the poem comes when Ephraim reveals that Jackson (DJ) is to be reborn again whereas JM is in his last life. While initially disconcerting, the effect of the announcement fades surprisingly quickly:

> The cloud passed
> More quickly than the shade it cast,
> Foreshadower of nothing, dearest heart,
> But the dim wish of lives to drift apart. (69)

Attraction revives for a moment as DJ describes Ephraim's stroking of Merrill in a dream, a scene that makes him feel a *"stab of the old possessiveness"* (71). The second half of the poem contains few appearances by Ephraim, though, an indication of a decline in the love which he symbolizes.

Section L is the pivotal section in "Ephraim," contrasting the summers of 1957 and 1974 so that the change in the relationship of JM and DJ becomes apparent. Amid the nostalgic image of the "Eisenhower grin" which compares well with the talk of Nixon's impeachment in 1974, amid the mellowness of Merrill's assertion that he and DJ had like "limbs thickening" lived on "in one another's shade" is the deadening note of attrition: "Life like the periodical not yet / Defunct kept hitting the stands" (84–85).

The waning of the love of JM and DJ is paralleled by the ailing of DJ's parents. The section ends with Merrill's painful, hypnotic reliving

of the death in South Africa of Rufus Farmetton, his previous incarnation, a further tilting of the poem in a downward direction. As if unable
to resolve the contrary feelings of Section L, Section M turns to other
subjects. 'M' stands for Maya Deren and for Myth. Deren's films and
her book, *Divine Horsemen,* incorporated her intuitive understanding of
a system of reincarnation comparable to that disclosed by Ephraim. In
Merrill's view, her life, including a momentous visit to Haiti where she
became caught up in mythological ritual, had a fruitful integrity in
which dream coalesced with film and both merged with the rest of her
experience.

The intellectual storehouses of Section O and Q effectively break the
narrative thread involving the relationship of JM and DJ. Section O,
which is set in Athens, contains reflections on the theme of evolution
that are relevant to the book's cosmology. The significance of the letter
'O' as a negation tends to weigh the section down with a sense of loss.
Everything of vitality, it seems to Merrill, is in the irrecoverable past.
In addition, the reader has become so accustomed to the absence of DJ
that a fleeting reference to him calling up the furnace repairman at the
end of the section comes as a shock. Section P is a portentous treatise on
power. Using a text and variations format, Merrill considers the running down of the universe on "warped, decelerating grooves" (98).
Ephraim makes a brief reappearance, but the vivacity of his earlier visits
has disappeared, and he is brushed aside by the massed quotations of
Sections Q.

The pedagogical neutrality of Section Q is in one sense symbolic of
the drying up of the poem's emotion. The quotations are nevertheless
important to the poem's themes. Merrill's favorite people are well
represented among those quoted: Maya Deren, Hans Lodeizen, Hera-
clitus, Proust, Auden, Spenser. The quotation from Maya Deren about
the crucial loss of vital myths in contemporary culture reinforces the
ominous allegory of Section P, which suggests that the present period
represents a twilight of the gods. The section is a philosophical and
historical rendering of the opening theme of the incarnation and
withdrawal of divinity from the world. Opposing the forces of dissolution are those few souls who have demonstrated their "USEFULNESS"
to the world, as Ephraim is quoted as saying, a small corps of extraordinary people whose wisdom, like that of the handful of just men in the
story of Sodom in *Genesis,* permits the world's survival (103). The

quotation from the Garden of Adonis section of Spenser's *Faerie Queene* is important in that it presents a model of the universe which is parallel to that set forth by Ephraim in which Eden is possible even within the context of time and mutability. Thus, in Section R, Merrill vows to "Leave to the sonneteer eternal youth" (109) and in Section S (which is named after Wallace Stevens) he presents the imagination as a counterweight to the draining of time.

The erosion of time is felt, though, in Section T, where Merrill recalls an incident in Proust that amplifies his own defeated sense of aging. Section U offers a Jungian view of the unconscious just before the poem reaches its brilliant coda in Section V, the walk through Venice. Here the theme of mutability, which has received philosophical treatment in the preceding sections, is given a concrete test in the image of the sinking and crumbling but still incomparably beautiful Renaissance city. Venice, like the Garden of Adonis in Section Q, is obviously subject to time and mutability. The degeneration of the Edenic city of Venice, has, rather like the decay of the relationship of JM and DJ, turned it into a kind of hell—

> Venise, pavane, nirvana, vice, wrote Proust
> Justly in his day. But in ours? The monumental
> "I" of stone—on top, an adolescent
> And his slain crocodile, both guano-white—
> Each visit stands for less. (119)

Venice appears to Merrill as a "whole heavenly city / Sinking, titanic ego mussel-blue" (119), a symbol simultaneously of both the greatness of man and of his narcissistic limitations. Those limitations are felt keenly by Merrill as he wanders disaffectedly through the city along with the invasion of tourists. The dominant imagery of the section contrasts the reality of the tourists' photographic films with the depth of the painters and sculptors whose works fill Venetian galleries and churches. The motif of *pentimento* returns to the poem in the reference to Giorgione's painting, the *Tempest*, which hangs in Venice and which X-rays have revealed conceals a mysterious, female moonbather beneath its top layer of paint. The painting's contrast of surfaces and depths arouses Merrill to consider the beauty that has been saved around him as well as that which has been lost. The incident fertilizes his imagination, and he produces a nacreous poem on a sudden squall that comes up. The fusion of air, water, and light is conveyed through the imagery of glassblowing, a traditional Venetian art. Under the sheet of rain the city seems "Vitrified in metamorphosis" (121).

The images mount until the scene resembles a sacred "monstrance clouded then like a blown fuse / If not a reliquary for St. James' / Vision of Life" (121). The hagiographic montage of St. Mark, patron of Venice, and *James* Merrill, spiritualistic devotee of the afterlife, crowns a series of impressions that unexpectedly reveal a pristine Merrill beneath the melancholy, rather jaded traveler. So too does the original vision of Venice survive beneath its faded, cracking surface. The city thus becomes a crucial test for Merrill, a "window fiery-mild, whose walked-through frame / Everything else, at sunset, hinged upon—" (121).

The dualism underlying Merrill's view of Venice is echoed in his unexpected encounter with his great-nephew, Wendell (Section W), who has been wandering through Europe as a student of art. Wendell's blunt rejection of his society ("sick, selfish, dumb as shit") ironically awakens Merrill's respect for man and civilization, for that in effect which Venice symbolizes (124). Not only was the city shaped by artists, but it attracted and nourished artists over the centuries, including Wagner and W. H. Auden, both of whom had played a part in Merrill's development as an artist. Auden collaborated with Igor Stravinsky and Chester Kallman in writing the libretto for *The Rake's Progress,* which was first performed in Venice in the 1950s. Merrill's friendship for Auden and Kallman, both dead now, becomes interfused with his golden memories of the opera to generate an image of a new Venice that rises "from the ashes of the High Baroque" (125). Furthermore, Merrill's remembrance that Wendell was "Ephraim's representative" in this life renews his sense that a design lurks beneath the surface of his own life. The impression becomes intense in Section X as he becomes gratefully conscious of the prevalence of female figures in his life— Maya-Maria-Kleo—and of the woman whose face lay beneath all of the others, that of his mother.

The poem ends in a postscript in which Merrill and Jackson, their traveling over with, take up residence again at the apartment in Stonington. The building is empty except for the two of them, and it is December: "Zero Week / Of the year's end" (34). The furnace is out again, as it had been in Athens, symbolizing the petering out of their relationship. The poem closes in a hush in which, ironically, neither can recall that anything in the apartment is missing—"nothing's gone, or nothing we recall" (136). Because the relationship has become tepid, carrying on with everyday life becomes painful. The poem closes sardonically in a no-man's land between hope and despair: "For here we are" (136). "The Book of Ephraim" is thereby completed even if emotionally unresolved. JM and DJ have reached a point of stasis just as the expiring year reaches its nadir.

"The Book of Ephraim" is heightened by a new, visionary strain in Merrill's writing which, even if it falls short of epic, surpasses the relatively modest boundaries of his earlier work. Furthermore, the poem is enriched by its lively erudition and burnished surface. Both imagery and versification contribute to the poem's attractive iridescence. Traditional forms, for example, ripple gracefully through the broad current of narrative. Section R is composed of five sonnets, which are disguised by being broken into quatrains and tercets; similarly, the meeting with Wendell (Section W) is enlivened by an exuberant display of terza rima. "The Book of Ephraim" is a significant poetic achievement, justifying the risk Merrill took when he decided to make art out of such improbable materials.

Mirabell

Mirabell: Books of Number (1978), the second part of Merrill's trilogy, won the National Book Award for 1979. The book, which runs to 182 pages, focuses on the relationship between science and culture. Regarding his intentions for *Mirabell*, Merrill has confided in an interview: "I think science is a visionary landscape in the twentieth century and was even in the nineteenth. . . . We certainly are starved for the scientific myths. These are constantly bursting out in front of us in fascinating forms, and I suppose the point would be to show or to somehow open the possibility that the classical myths and the scientific myths are really one and the same."[4] The poem centers on the contrast between the desperate state of the world—again highlighting the problems of nuclear weaponry and overpopulation—and the vast potentialities of science.

Merrill had been leafing through books like Isaac Asimov's *Guide to Science* and Lewis Thomas's *Lives of a Cell* in search of a vocabulary and some possible images for his poems of science. He had been convinced for some time that scientific ideas, like any other ideas, depended on "metaphor, ways of talking," and thus liked to think poets might be useful in the discussions of scientific knowledge that dominate contemporary learning.[5] He intended as well to provide in one of the books of the trilogy a model of reality that at least purports to be objective, as *Mirabell*'s deterministic theme of "NO ACCIDENT" indicates (82). Number is the fundamental principle of structuring in *Mirabell*. The books or chapters of *Mirabell* are numbered 0 to 9 with subsections being divided in the same manner. The sequence suggests an arrival at a new level in the spiral of knowledge at the end of each book. The importance of the number "0" is underscored by the fact that it resembles the atom, the central symbol in *Mirabell*. The "O" signifies both positive and negative energy, both the fullness of being and the lurking opposition of antimatter.

Most things in *Mirabell* are given mathematical significance. For example, the book's presiding spirit, "741" (later named Mirabell), symbolizes among other things the union of the quartet of central characters—Merrill (JM), Jackson (DJ), Maria Mitsotaki, and W. H. Auden. The penetration of the book's system of numbering can be seen in the way in which language is turned to numerical purpose, as in Book O, which begins with the word "Oh" or Book 1, which begins with the phrase "UNHEEDFULL-ONE" (3, 19). At the same time the interfusion of number and language underscores Merrill's belief in the unity of science with the rest of culture. Nonetheless, science's particular emphasis is on objectivity, which number, unburdened by connotations, symbolizes.

Consistent with the overall stress on number, the versification is quantitative, the revelations from the spirit world coming in eye-straining, uppercase, fourteen syllable lines. As most of *Mirabell* is composed of communications from the afterlife, the poem looks as if it had been composed on a teletype machine. The intent is again to silhouette the voice of science—unwavering, assertive, direct. The human participants in *Mirabell* use a more varied, ten-beat line.

If on the one hand Merrill created in *Mirabell* a myth of a universal past that encompassed science, art, philosophy, and religion, he also constructed a bright comedy of manners. *Mirabell* is almost all dialogue, and much of it, fortunately, is silkily light and provocative. Mirabell, the book's presiding spirit, is given a name from Congreve's Restoration comedy, *The Way of the World,* a play that, like Merrill's poem, thrives on the repartee of a small, elite cast of sophisticates. Even heaven is presented as a drawing-room in which good manners prevail, as can be seen in the reception given David Jackson's mother by one of his dead friends:

> Marius Bewley, who once gave her tea
> Eighteen years ago on Staten Island,
> Takes Mary up. Reads her the Wordsworth *Ode,*
> Pours out the steeping innocence she craves. (9)

Merrill's blending of witty dialogue and themes of high seriousness is consistent with his reluctance to make any ideas sacrosanct. He describes his use of scientific terminology at one point, for example, as just a "touch fishy when the tide is low" (162). On another occasion he fears that his cosmological myth may be nothing but "Warmed-up Milton, Dante, Genesis" (42). Counter to the poem's ingrained skepticism, however, is a tenacious gnosticism, a belief that man must *know* in order to survive. Thus, Merrill's suppression of his customary verbal splendour in *Mirabell* was intended to divert attention from the language to the message. "For me," he has said, the "talk and the tone—along with the elements of plot—are the candy coating. The pill itself is another matter. The reader who can't swallow it has my full sympathy. I've choked on it again and again."[6]

The poem opens in the present time, the summer of 1976. Mirroring man's inevitable, bicameral view of things, the setting is divided between the domed dining-room seen in "The Book of Ephraim" and an adjoining room. The colors of the rooms roughly stand for power and passion (red) and wisdom and order (blue). A mirror is placed near the Ouija board so that visiting spirits may peer in at the two mediums, who have overcome the emotional impasse in their relationship reached at the end of "The Book of Ephraim." During the poem, JM and DJ buy a carpet, whose design features "limber, leotarded, blue-eyed bats / —Symbols of eternity, said the dealer" (4). New dark blue wallpaper extends the bat design, laying the allegorical foundation for the dark

angels who eventually hover over the poem. Foreground action is kept
to a minimum: DJ's parents die; JM visits megalithic ruins in England;
DJ goes to Boston for a hernia operation. The outside world is glimpsed
just briefly enough to stabilize the two mediums, reminding them that
they are still of this world.

There are three levels of discourse in the poem, the human (JM and
DJ), the dead (Maria and Auden as chief spokesmen), and the dark, bat
angels. Discussion ranges from the "vast to the microscopic," as Merrill
put it in a later note,[7] and from abstruse speculation to piquant drollery
(Plato is pictured in drag in Book 3). *Mirabell*'s underlying dualism is so
pervasive, moreover, that even the book's hilarious sexual intrigues
have their serious side. Homosexuality, for example, is associated with
a psychological receptivity that is said to make JM and DJ superior
subjects for cosmic revelations (60).

The relationship of Merrill and Jackson to Auden and Maria is
essentially filial, Auden being a mentor/father while Maria is an earth
mother. "Strange about parents," Merrill has commented in connection
with Auden's and Maria's role in the poem, "we have such easy access to
them and such daunting problems of communication. Over the Ouija
board it was just the other way. A certain apparatus was needed to get in
touch—but then! Affection, understanding, tact, surprises, laughter,
tears."[8] In addition, of course, Maria and Auden fulfill roles similar to
those played by Virgil and Beatrice in Dante's *Divine Comedy*.

Each of the central actors speaks in a distinctive voice so that one is
rarely in doubt about who is speaking even when, as is often the case,
they are not introduced. Auden usually addresses JM and DJ as "My
Dears" while Maria calls them "Mes Enfants"; Ephraim characteristically begins by saying "Mes Chers"; JM and DJ usually refer to Maria as
"Mama."

Maria's is the most poignant story in *Mirabell*. Her painful death by
cancer, which involved radiation therapy, has, it is disclosed, jeopar-
dized her soul. Tearfully, JM and DJ learn that she is destined to
become a plant. In the meantime, however, her role, which reflects her
familiarity with politics, is to *plant* guilt "FLEURS DE MAUVAISE
CONSCIENCE / In politicians' beds" (8). Gardening motifs are used
throughout *Mirabell* and *Scripts* to identify Maria. The underlying
meaning of her becoming a plant is, of course, one of the poem's
concessions to the bitter literalness of death.

Consistent with the overall structure of ascent in the trilogy, the revelations in *Mirabell* represent a higher, more reliable version of reality than that obtained in "The Book of Ephraim." Thus, the system of reincarnation outlined in the earlier book, while not denied, is seen in *Mirabell* to occupy a relatively minor place in the overall running of the cosmos. Reincarnations proceed in *Mirabell*—the most startling being Chester Kallman's rebirth in Africa as a heterosexual, black political leader—but the focus of the book lies elsewhere. Furthermore, some of Ephraim's earlier revelations are described merely as useful fictions for initiating JM and DJ into the lower mysteries.

As is true of the trilogy in general, *Mirabell* concerns itself with time and mutability and its dominant motif is that of metamorphosis. Darkness, guilt, and grief join with images of ascending consciousness to suggest a Dantean purgatory, a place of pain where the soul is refined into glory in much the same way as the bat spirit, 741, is changed into a peacock in the course of the book.

741's account of history, which appears to be a mixture of Milton and Tolkien, tells of a world originally inhabited by a lower race of centaurs, who in turn created a race of higher intellects like himself. Antagonism results, and the angelic intellects eventually build a space world that is attached to the ground by anchored cables. Through neglect the anchor points disintegrate, and the angelic world ends in catastrophe, as does the race of centaurs. The dark angels of *Mirabell,* reminiscent of the fallen angels in *Paradise Lost,* fall because of a proud aloofness from the physical world. They are followed by the creation of a race of white angels who are described in detail in *Scripts for the Pageant*. In *Mirabell* the power of the white angels is felt from time to time in interventions that interrupt the relay of information from the dark angels, who appear to be atoning for past transgressions. The extent of these transgressions becomes magnified by the suggestion that they had misused the power of the atom, as contemporary man appears to be on the verge of doing.

The darkness of *Mirabell* is offset by a view of the control center of the universe—the Research Lab—where key, selected figures do "V" work (130). The Roman numeral stands for the five immortals whose spirits cycle through history and who essentially keep the world from coming apart. Individual manifestations of these spirits include luminaries like Plato, Galileo, Blake, and Einstein as well as lesser known people like Merrill's scientist friend, George Cotzias.

Allegorically, 741's history of the world documents man's cultural evolution from a simple agrarianism to the advanced technology of the atomic age. The richness of *Mirabell* lies in Merrill's compressed stacking of allusiveness within symbolic types like the bat angels. The angels simultaneously represent prehistoric creatures, the instability of matter, and intellectual pride. While the dark angels symbolize the explosive, evolving forces within matter that constituted the chief peril to life in the past, man is now viewed as the principal threat to the cosmos. Underlying the conflict between evolution and antimatter— the terms for the struggle between order and chaos in *Mirabell*—is the presence of nature itself, the ground of being. Nature, or Queen Mum—as it is called in the trilogy—is portrayed as possessing a protective wisdom that has rescued life thus far. However, man's increasing control over nature impedes its wise, corrective action, making it imperative that he learn something of that wisdom. Hence, the classroom format of *Mirabell* and *Scripts for the Pageant.*

The poem opens, appropriately enough, with a view of prehistory in Merrill's visit to the archeological sites of Stonehenge and Avebury in England. The stone monoliths of Avebury, with their circular design, conform to the 'O' which titles this section of the poem:

> It's both a holy and a homely site
> Slowlier perfused than eye can see
> (Whenever the stones blink a century
> Blacks out) by this vague track
> Of brick and thatch and birdsong any June
> Galactic pollen will have overstrewn. (18)

The lines suggest the great vistas of time and space that underlay the formation of the planet, the image of "Galactic pollen" being especially far reaching in suggesting both the present vegetative overgrowth of the past and the fertilizing of the earth itself out of cosmic matter in the distant past. More significantly, the scene also suggests the orderly procession of matter through time, an unfolding that may be abruptly terminated—the poem will make clear—by man.

741's arrival at the Ouija board to persuade Merrill to write "POEMS OF SCIENCE" is an attempt by nature (acting through the subconscious minds of JM and DJ) to awaken man to the precarious history of life (19). 741 is thus a dour familiar spirit in comparison with the rather convivial Ephraim. He speaks from "WITHIN THE ATOM" delivering an appeal from matter itself to be spared man's recklessly and potentially catastrophic ignorance (19). The only force that can compete with the volatile energy of matter is that of mind, which alone can "SHOW MAN THE WAY TO PARADISE" (20). The problem is that the antithetical negative and positive forces that drive the atom and all matter are also mirrored in the mind of man. The poem thus portrays man as at a crossroads where his management of nature has reached the point at which he will either go under, taking all of life with him, or move up the evolutionary ladder. "THE NEXT RACE WILL BE OF GODS," 741 predicts dispassionately (23). Although scientifically detached until his transformation into a peacock, 741 holds out hope for man by emphasizing the fruitfulness of history as a cumulative process: "NOTHING IS EVER EVER LOST   THE WATERFALL WILL HOLD / YR 2 BRIGHT DROPS & YOU WILL SPLASH INTO THE GREAT CLEAR POOL" (23). 741 thus presents his listeners with a cultural application of the first law of thermodynamics.

The path of wisdom in *Mirabell* lies not in taking prudent charge of nature but in recognizing the wisdom that is already immanent in nature. This is the meaning of Maria's reentry into the life cycle as a plant and of Auden's later reentry as a stone. Both events symbolize the interpenetration of mind and matter. The story of the Egyptian pharoah, Akhenaton (spelled Akhnaton by 741) also underlines the union of mind and matter. Akhenaton and his sister/wife Nefertiti began a revolutionary, monotheistic religion in ancient Egypt that was based on the sun. In terms of the development of civilization Merrill pictures Akhenaton as a major, original force, and portrays him in the poem as one of the immortal five who do V work. Merrill alters the history of Akhenaton, however, to include an ill-fated, ancient experiment with nuclear energy. The alteration moves the poem's two symbols of sun and atom closer together so that the traditional, historical symbol of power, the sun, is directly linked with the foremost symbol of power in the contemporary world. Furthermore, the imagination and consciousness are eventually identified with the sun ("S/O/L"), further confirming the interfusion of mind and matter (166).

Thus, in an ambitious intellectual synthesis reminiscent of Blake, Merrill creates a unified field of religion and science which carries the inescapable inference that man, God, and matter are one and the same. Hence, when Merrill pictures Dante as being blinded by the omnipotent, whirling ring of light in the *Paradiso,* he understands the scene to mean that Dante was looking into the "ATOM'S EYE" wherein he saw the "POTENTIAL OF PARADISE" (38). The atom in *Mirabell* symbolizes the capacity for boundless creativity as readily as it signifies irrevocable destruction. It also signifies the power historically locked up in art, religion, and science. Because power is distributed through mind as well as matter, or rather through mind in matter, the artist with his knowledge of language and symbol is as potent a force in shaping the future as any other.

The future hinges most critically, however, on those like the five immortals whose souls have density—"Human uranium," as it is called at one point (44). For their contribution to the development of Western culture Merrill uses the Jews as a metaphor for souls of great density. Analogously, the souls of the characters in *Mirabell* are assessed in terms of their value, Auden's being described as platinum, Merrill's silver, Jackson's a mixture of silver and tin, and so on, the metallurgical imagery conforming to the scientific motifs that dominate the book. Merrill divides history into a mass of benighted souls destined for nature's vast compost heap and a minority of enlightened souls whose spiritual continuity essentially constitutes civilization. His aristocratic division of life, a secular, impersonal version of the Last Judgment, is consistent with the neutrality of viewpoint in *Mirabell,* a poem about hard truths. The atmosphere of urgency in the poem arises from the fact that through the windfall of technology unprecedented power has fallen in recent times into the "HANDS OF ANIMALS SOULS," a melancholy reflection on the state of contemporary political leadership (52).

The metamorphosis of 741 from an emotionally inert, cosmic messenger into a blushingly ardent peacock symbolizes the need for more than wisdom. The transformation follows 741's observation of JM and DJ, whose love eventually warms him into life emotionally. Affection in *Mirabell* stabilizes relationships in much the same way that the molecule is depicted as stabilizing the "dance" of atoms so that matter can acquire form (66). In addition, in spite of the purgatorial scenario of *Mirabell,* the poem affirms that heaven lies just beyond man's conventional line of vision: "PARADISE   ARCADIA SURROUNDS US UNREALIZED/ FILLING EACH OF US FOR THE LENGTH OF A LOVE OR A THOUGHT" (71). The same holds true for man's conventional view of time: "WHAT U CALL FUTURE WE CALL REALITY" (82). These perceptions cut through the poem's linear emphasis on biological and cultural evolution to suggest a paradise that is accessible in the present given a change of vision. Thus, JM and DJ are told that a God B (Biology) is not "HISTORY / BUT EARTH ITSELF   HE IS THE GREENHOUSE" (93). The greenhouse is Merrill's scientifically neutral image for the life process, an image that allows for pastoral, Edenic overtones but does not require them. The realization of such overtones depends utterly on what man does to nature and to himself, and this in turn depends upon the quality of his vision.

Mirabell's reiterated theme of "NO ACCIDENT" raises the harrowing question of the value of the poem's dire revelations if everything in the universe is predetermined (82). The extent of the determinism surfaces in an inset poem in which Merrill considers with refreshing concreteness the chain of causality underlying his own existence. He begins by visualizing his parents' courtship:

> The parlor, Jacksonville.
> Lamplight through the glass transom
> Stained to some final visibility
> Like tissue on a slide—as,
> Hole by pre-punched hole,
> From the magnolia tree
> Outpoured the mockingbird's
> Player-piano roll . . . (101)

The bitterness underlying Merrill's choice of a mockingbird is intensified by the mechanical determinism implied by the player-piano image. By the same token, though, his life has been immeasurably enriched, he sees, by his equally deterministic attraction to friends like Maria, Auden, and David Jackson.

While the underlying determinism of life is never refuted in the poem—though not for want of trying by JM and DJ—man is praised in general for his capacity for resistance to the conditions he finds himself in. A portentous example of man's penchant for resistance, however, is his resistance to that nature of which he is a part. This unfortunate resistance springs from his cerebral lack of respect for the physical world around him: "MAN WANTS IMMORTALITY & NATURE WANTS

MANURE" (135). The task of art as the successor to religion is to mediate between mind and nature and also between science and culture.

The mood of the poem lightens toward the end as the quartet of JM, DJ, Maria, Auden plan a picnic. They also prepare themselves for a visit from one of the mysterious white angels who will be the subject of the next volume. All that remains of Mirabell is a little dime-store peacock made of tin with a broken, mechanical tail (173). The image symbolizes Mirabell's obsolescence now that he has delivered his message. The poem's participants now look to heaven for fresh revelations. As if preparing for a sacrament, JM and DJ fast before receiving their effulgent visitor:

> A whole day without drink or nicotine;
> Then how, tomorrow afternoon, to DRESS
> THE MIND in slow transparencies of blue,
> Red, yellow, and green;
> Approaching, beyond anxiousness,
> The round white tabletop—in sight of it
> A single candle lit,
> And nature's worldwide effigy before
> Our eyes—to think of Water, Earth, Air, Fire,
> And of each other. (176–77)

The colors stand for particular ways of seeing which together constitute the full spectrum, the white light that is expected to emanate from above. The allusion to the elements indicates that JM and DJ will attend their heavenly visitor in a conscious communion with nature. The lyricism of this section is a sign that Merrill was moving away from the scientific pedagogy of *Mirabell* to the visionary raptures of *Scripts for the Pageant*. The figure of Michael, "GUARDIAN OF THE LIGHT," materializes imperceptibly out of the softness and sheen of Long Island Sound, which Merrill has been looking at (182). Michael's brief message reaffirms the intimacy of mind and matter with new force: "GOD IS THE ACCUMULATED INTELLIGENCE IN CELLS SINCE THE DEATH OF THE FIRST DISTANT CELL" (182). The cell and its genetic treasures will be the major motif of *Scripts* just as the atom was in *Mirabell*.

Although Merrill makes some attempt to provide a personal framework for the revealed text of *Mirabell*, arguing that the poem feeds on its "personages' lives," the final effect of the poem is expository (124). Although on one level Mirabell and his revelations are simply effusions of the relationship between JM and DJ, the poem nonetheless has a markedly impersonal character in comparison with both "The Book of Ephraim" and *Scripts for the Pageant,* a reflection of its didactic purpose and eclectic, scientific superstructure. There are moments when the poetry brilliantly overtakes the theorizing, as in the lyric interlude in which Mercury as god of the mirror is celebrated in Book 8. Moreover, the verse, other than that used for Mirabell's revelations, is as supple and felicitous as ever—with Merrill turning with facility from sonnet to villanelle and from terza rima to blank verse as if these forms were as natural as speech. On the whole, though, the arias are few, and the recitative long. The sense of setting is also tenuous, not because of the occult medium, but because the message is pressing. Nonetheless, *Mirabell* succeeds as part of Merrill's prodigious trilogy, whose momentum carries the book with its particular scientific aura.

Scripts for the Pageant

Scripts for the Pageant (1980), the final volume of the trilogy, runs to 235 pages. Although there are new characters and the situations of existing characters change, the principal difference between *Scripts* and *Mirabell* is atmospheric. Suffused with a diaphanous light, as opposed to the darkness of *Mirabell, Scripts for the Pageant* possesses a mellow, visionary fullness. Merrill's 'final' vision in *Scripts* turns out to be a vision of possibilities. There are three possible scripts for the pageant of the future entitled "Yes," "&," and "No." In a sense the tripartite structure condenses that of the whole trilogy. The spirit of affirmation is more pronounced in *Scripts for the Pageant* than in the other volumes, for example, just as that of negation is strongest in "The Book of Ephraim"; *Mirabell* strikes a balance between hope and defeat. While Merrill is obviously skeptical about the classical hierarchy of heaven, hell, and purgatory—as well as of immortality, for that matter—each of the three books exudes something of the atmosphere and symbolism of its Dantean prototype.

The cast in *Scripts* again features the quartet of JM, DJ, Maria, and W. H. Auden. The quartet is augmented by performances from the recently deceased Robert Morse—Merrill's musical friend from Stonington who had appeared as Andrew in "The Summer People"—

and George Cotzias, the microbiologist whom Merrill met in the 1970s. The white angels are the star performers, though—Michael, the angel of light, Emmanuel, the water angel, Raphael, the earth angel, and Gabriel, the angel of fire and death. The apotheosis of nature, which Merrill had begun in *Braving the Elements,* is thus completed in *Scripts.* Nature herself presides benevolently over the poem in the form of Queen Mum, a hybrid character who combines the role of earth mother played by Maria—and Shelley's ethereal Queen Mab. Merrill employs tetrameter for the quartet of JM, DJ, Maria, and Auden, while choosing an ampler but still flexible pentameter for the angels. Scenes are frequently rounded off in rhyme as in Shakespeare.

The difference in vantage point between *Scripts for the Pageant* and the preceding volumes of the trilogy can be seen in the appearance of a unicorn named Unice (usually called Uni), a *uni*que descendant from an earlier Edenic world. The metamorphosis of the centaur of *Mirabell* into the unicorn of *Scripts* underlines the idyllic character of the later book. The elevated mood of *Scripts* can also be seen in the eventual, joyful revelation of Maria as a reincarnation of Plato and finally as an incarnation of nature (Queen Mum) in which role she appears translucently robed as Mary (Maria), queen of heaven.

Accompanying the sublimation of earlier characters and motifs is the underlying dialectical opposition embedded in the poem's three subtitles. The tension between Michael, whose spirit dominates the 'Yes' section, and Gabriel, whose outlook dominates 'No,' is the most dramatic example of the book's many polarizations. Unlike his practice in *Mirabell* Merrill never permits the argument in *Scripts* to pull away from the human situation that underlies it. Similarly, more attention is paid to scene setting, and in some cases—as in the description of the island of Samos—the poetry reaches new heights in freshness and coloring. The poem moves from Stonington to Athens and then on to Venice, and the foreground is always firmly present in the reader's consciousness. The interweaving of communications from the afterlife with the movement of life in the foreground is vividly apparent in the scene in which Merrill, alone at his desk in Stonington, attempts to put his spiritualistic transcriptions into some kind of order:

> Quarries from the transcript murky blocks
> Of revelation, now turning a phrase
> To catch the red sunset, now up at dawn

> Edging into place a paradox—
> One atop the other; and each weighs
> More than he can stop to think. Despair
> Alternates with insighr. Strange how short
> The days have grown, considering the vain
> Ticking, back, forth, of leafless metronomes
> Beyond the pane, where atmosphere itself
> One morning crystallizes. Winter's here. (15–16)

Even the transcriptions from the spirit world seem more palatable than in *Mirabell,* not only because of their contents but because the speakers are more eloquent. Similarly, although JM and DJ continue to be entombed within their absorbing communion with the dead most of the time, even that obsession appears less stifling and more resplendent a condition than it did in *Mirabell*:

> *The schoolroom stretches to a line. It breaks*
> *Cleverly into two floating poles*
> *Of color that in dark 'air' glow and pulse,*
> *Undulate and intertwine like snakes.*
> *Whatever road we travel now, this twinned*
> *Emblem lights, and is both distant guide*
> *And craft we're sealed hermetically inside,*
> *Winged as by fever through the shrieking wind.* (54)

What Merrill evidently wanted and what he achieved was the texture of Dante's *Paradiso* in which all of the images are shot through with the light of heaven. Everything in *Scripts for the Pageant* is beautifully visualized so that even the most furtive abstractions enter fully clothed, as can be seen in the stage directions for the entry of Psyche, the *"third and fairest face of Nature,"* in the "&" section:

> *Enter—in a smart white summer dress,*
> *Ca. 1900, discreetly bustled,*
> *Trimmed if at all with a fluttering black bow;*
> *Black ribbon round her throat; a cameo;*
> *Gloved but hatless.* (125)

The emotional temperature of *Scripts* also surpasses that of *Mirabell.* JM and DJ sink into melancholy at the thought that Maria might have committed suicide; Auden weeps at the beauty of JM's verses; JM and

DJ draw introspectively into a deep love for their joint history, whose unfolding has never been so intensely appreciated despite their all too visible aging. Emerging from the purgatorial crucible of *Mirabell,* JM asks at the beginning of *Scripts*: "are we now washed crystalline?" (3). In mute reply JM is observed to have a heavenly radiance surrounding him (23) that covers DJ as well in spite of the incongruity of their "old clothes, / Wrinkle and graying hair and liver spot" (14).

Michael, in blazing white light, appropriately presides over the "Yes" section, the motto of which is: "NEVER DISAPPROVE   IT WARPS THE SOUL" (74). The dominant symbol is that of the cell, the "STRUCTURELESS STRUCTURE OF THE SOUL CELL, OR MORE PROPERLY THE SUBLIME STRUCTURE OF THE CELLS OF GOD BIOLOGY'" (8). Mirabell, called back to relay further instruction, describes the elegance of the cell:

PALATIAL   THE VEG CELLS LUMINOUS,
THE MINERAL FIERY   BOTH HOT AND COLD FIRE. THESE
GENIUS STRUCTURES OF THE MASTER ARCHITECT HAVE THE
SUPREME QUALITY OF WEIGHTLESS DOMES   THEIR ELABO-
RATE
GROINING & VITAL PILLARS POSITIOND WITHOUT BASEWORK,
FOR BOTH ROOF & FLOOR BREATHE LIFE & HOLD TO EACH
OTHER BY TRANSLUCENT MEANS. (8)

The cell is Merrill's symbol for an interdependent and interpenetrable universe in which all that exists, even the basest mineral, exists as part of a sentient, precious whole. Life's star, though, is "INTELLIGENCE . . . THE SOURCE OF LIGHT," as Michael explains, adding: "FEAR NOTHING WHEN / YOU STAND IN IT   I RAISE YOU UP AMONG US HAIL   HAIL" (14).

The serenity and confidence of the "Yes" section are balanced, as always in Merrill, by motifs that have a counter spin, here the dying of George Cotzias and the ominous presence of Gabriel. In part Gabriel symbolizes enormous destructive power, like the volatile, nuclear energy that had been figured in *Mirabell*: "I ROSE, A SKY OF BURSTING ATOMS" (34). He also represents the dark passions within the psyche ("YOUR BLOOD, YOUR LIFE")—the revolt of the body and subconscious, here liberated from their rather cringing roles in *Mirabell*. He also proclaims himself the "FOREVER SWINGING

GATE BETWEEN LIFE & HEAVEN" (34). Given his role as a font of destructive power, the language is ambiguous to say the least. He clarifies his function, however, by describing himself as the "OTHER SIDE" of God B's V work (34). At best, then, he represents an annihilating force that sweeps away deadwood in the path of evolution; at worst he constitutes a threat to life itself. Later in the poem he is described as having inherited one of nature's black genes. The characterization of Gabriel is suitably complex, his face resembling Lucifer's one moment and then fading to reemerge as the shy lord of antimatter. He is consistently portrayed, though, as a dark fire opposed to Michael's light. God B (nature) is the "BALANCER OF CHAOS & CREATION" in "Yes," mediating between Michael and Gabriel, order and chaos, reason and energy (40).

Emmanuel, the spirit of water, refreshes and renews man, bringing him hope and leaving a trail of reflective pools for his memory to follow even to his evolutionary beginnings in the primeval sea. Raphael, the spirit of earth, is equally supportive to man: "O GREEN SPRING EARTH, O WITTY WITH HOPE" (65). Merrill's explanation in an unpublished interview of why he pictured the earth as "witty" reveals the baroque filigree of his mind. He thought of the earth as witty "in the sense that it forms gems. Then Michael says something about gravity as a characteristic of cosmic dust and it seemed to me that there was something I read about—I don't know, maybe just the tininess of those particles, those original particles, were they short-lived?"[9] Brevity is the connection, then, the proverbial source of wit.

Merrill's divinizing of the four elements was designed to revitalize contemporary man's sense of the miracle of being. He lamented the desiccated image of divinity which theologians and artists had constructed in recent centuries:

> the past two or three
> Hundred years have seen a superhuman
> All-shaping Father dwindle (as in Newman)
> To ghostly, disputable Essence or
> Some shaggy-browed, morality-play bore
> (As in the Prologue to *Faust*). Today the line
> Drawn is esthetic. One allows divine
> Discourse, if at all, in paraphrase. (66)

Merrill's God and Merrill's heaven are culminations of both the beauty
and the facts of existence portrayed in "The Book of Ephraim" and
Mirabell, a bracing synthesis of Darwin and Plato: "EFFICIENCY IS
WELDED HERE / TO BEAUTY AS THE SOUL IS TO SURVIVAL"
(63).

The "Yes" section ends with Auden's haunting picture of God B
singing alone into the universe "KEEPING UP HIS NERVE ON A
LIFERAFT" (80). The vulnerability of Merrill's God derives from his
isolation, which reflects the fragmentation and alienation of mind and
matter, and from man's loss of the sense of divinity. Listening to
Auden's impressions, Merrill reflects:

> Dante saw
> The Rose in fullest bloom. Blake saw it sick.
> You and Maria, who have seen the bleak
> Unpetalled knob, must wonder: will it last
> Till spring? Is it still rooted in the Sun? (81)

The "&" section opens with a poem about Merrill's arrival by boat on
the historic Greek island of Samos. The island was the birthplace of
Pythagoras, the Greek mathematician and philosopher whose synthesis
of mathematics and conduct antedated Merrill's own attempt to unite
science, art, and religion into a single model of culture. The night
sea-passage offers a transfigured view of the commingled elements of
earth, air, fire, and water:

> And still, at sea all night, we had a sense
> Of sunrise, golden oil poured upon water,
> Soothing its heave, letting the sleeper sense
> What inborn, amniotic homing sense
> Was ferrying him—now through the dream-fire
> In which (it has been felt) each human sense
> Burns, now through ship's radar's cool sixth sense,
> Or mere unerring starlight—to an island.
> Here we were. The twins of Sea and Land,
> Up and about for hours—hues, cries, scents—
> Had placed at eye level a single light
> Croissant: the harbor glazed with warm pink light. (87)

The passage is a superb example of Merrill's power and grace in *Scripts
for the Pageant.* The apotheosis of the elements is not simply a raising of

nature but a redefining of heaven, an appeal for a vision of life as a translucent gauze in which matter and mind, form and spirit, heaven and hell are dissolved in a sublime unity.

The lectures in "&" are delivered by Maria, Auden, George Cotzias, and Robert Morse. The ample humanity of these speakers raises them all to a level comparable with the angels, although, like the angelic throng, which includes the dark figure of Gabriel, these human lecturers have had a shadow thrown across their lives, that of death. The axis of life and death is vividly portrayed in the life of George Cotzias whose microbiological experiments hold the promise of greater longevity for all men while he himself has died prematurely of cancer. The theme of "&" is thus appropriately "EQUIVOCAL," as Auden puts it: "ON A CRUST SO FRAGILE / IT NEEDS GOD'S CONSTANT VIGIL TO KEEP US AFLOAT" (109). In keeping with the visionary spaciousness of *Scripts*, the soul—that which life most crucially hinges upon—is described by Cotzias, the voice of science in the poem, as potent "NONGENETIC / STUFF" (93). Cotzias's remark points to the presence in the genetic pool of an evolving, ingrained will for perfection that eludes the microscope, a consciousness within nature itself of a "GRAND DESIGN" (93).

Maria's lecture centers on the origins of the universe. Her affinity to plant life makes her sensitive to the immanent purpose in matter which Cotzias hypothesizes about. She therefore associates vegetation with activities usually attributed to higher levels of being—as in her observation that the "FAMILY OF MOSS, / ESTABLISHED A TACTILE LANGUAGE" (107). In line with Merrill's practice of clothing every idea, Maria's verdant view of the cosmos colors the whole of the foreground:

> *The company has entered, come to order.*
> *One new touch only—in the carpet's border*
> *A vine-meander, yesterday unseen,*
> *Is now distinct, spring shades of blue and green.* (108)

In his lecture Auden attempts to bridge the worlds of art and science by contending that great poets, for example, have always been stimulated not by abstractions but by concrete facts. Referring to Blake, he sketches the transmutations of scientific fact into poetic and religious vision:

THE ATOMS OF DEMOCRITUS, THE BRIGHT
DANCE OF NEWTON'S PARTICLES SO THRILLED
HIS MIND, THAT A GREAT POET FILLED
THE TENTS OF ISRAEL WITH LIGHT. (109)

Cotzias's lecture with its scientific orientation contrasts with the
comparative subjectivity of the lectures by Auden and Maria. His
subject is matter, which he describes as a paste that results from the
meshing of atoms spinning in opposite directions. Cotzias portrays
matter as a dynamic balance between the dissolution and recovery of
form. Appropriately, a dialectical motif colors the foreground during
his lecture:

> *The carpet's ground, revived, now glows*
> *A dark rose—at whose center, black on white,*
> *What is that thornscript firman or mandala*
> *Teasingly sharp? On George's brow still wet*
> *A mirror gleams drilled by a black eye-hole:*
> *Diagnostic emblem of the soul.* (116)

The contredanse of atoms within the molecule is mirrored in the
structure of the mind, as the passage suggests, just as it is also
duplicated in the macrocosm where antimatter lurks in antithetical
balance with matter.

In section "&" balance is everything. James Merrill and George
Cotzias balance each other as poles of art and science which together
constitute a whole sensibility and a whole knowledge. In parallel
fashion the goddess, Psyche, is described by Michael as the "TWIN
SISTER TO OUR GOD BIOLOGY" (125). The awkwardness that
results when the mind isolates itself artificially from matter is humorously illustrated in the scene in which JM and DJ sun themselves on
rocks along the Aegean. Jackson proposes the hypothetical difficulty of
attempting to describe a chair without alluding to its use. Merrill
ponders the question:

> —just deduce
> As best one can the abstract entity.
> The mind on hunkers, squinting *not* to see,
> Gives up. Who needs this hypothetical
> Instrument of torture anyway? (124)

The "&" section closes with a familiar Merrill symbol, a "final waterfall" which draws toward itself the "earthward flow / Of Paradise" (144). As always in *Scripts for the Pageant* Merrill links his cosmological themes with the foreground action so that the faith in being which is articulated in the section is echoed in the lives of JM and DJ with their "love, trust, need" for each other (144). The foreground surfaces with limpid clarity in the serenely beautiful final poem of the section, "The House in Athens." Merrill's house and its surroundings—"Sky, mountain, monastery, / Traffic blur and glint / From center town"— are here perceived not as a distraction from a more engrossing encounter with a world of spirits but rather as the very flower of being (150). Looking out over waving oleander on their terrace, he and Jackson contentedly consider—for the moment, at any rate—the heaven they have made out of their lives.

Gabriel dominates the "No" section, arguing for the usefulness of mutability and death. That usefulness could ultimately require, he argues, the extinction of the human race should man threaten the survival of the planet. The ominousness of Merrill's portrait of Gabriel is intensified by his knowledge that the antimatter which Gabriel symbolizes has already been proven to exist in the laboratory.[10] The analogous presence of antimatter in human history is symbolized by the faces of Hitler and Caligula, which float through the chalky darkness of this section to illustrate man's inherited, apparently incorrigible addiction to destructiveness. Merrill's deceased friends, Cotzias, Maria, and Auden intervene on behalf of human life to argue against Gabriel's triumphantly logical vision of man's inevitable disappearance. Cotzias attributes the destructiveness of human beings to their myopic attraction to "EVEN OUR SHORT BRUTISH LIVES" (157). A further complication is the pernicious effect of man's demythologizing of his culture, as Psyche points out: "TIME WITHOUT GOD OR NATURE   RUNNING WILD / IN THE BAD DREAMS & BRAINCELLS OF ITS CHILD" (158). A Gothic pageant of fear and evil surges within man's behavior precisely because the spiritual dimensions of his life are unacknowledged.

Maria, whose hopeful green cuts through the ghostly dark, appeals to Gabriel on the ground that man's curiosity is his glory and that the life process would thus be impoverished without him. Conceding that this same curiosity can unleash man's destructiveness, she argues nonetheless that the benefits outweigh the risk. Here again, one finds

evidence of the durable gnosticism that underlies Merrill's poem: evil is
blindness; goodness is seeing.

Aiding Maria as a symbolic counterweight in this section is the
procession of religious founders—Buddha, Christ, Mohammed—all of
whom initially lift the oppressive darkness of this part of the "No"
section. Their impact on history, however, is depicted as a visionary
flash followed by a settling darkness as their followers misinterpret and
vulgarize their original inspiration.

Merrill softens the symmetrical clash of darkness and light in a
passage about the brain:

> WHO LENT BRAIN-MATTER ITS PROVERBIAL GRAY?
> AND PRESSES NOW AGAINST THE WHITE OF MIND
> UNLIMITED   UNREPULSED LIGHT   THE BLINDING
> REVEILLE: IMAGINATION   METAPHOR
> SHATTERED BY WHITE REASON! IS THE BLACK
> HOLE A REFUGE? (165)

Faced with the blinding light of reality, which finally shines here as it
does in Dante, man is pictured as groping for the security of his native
gray or for a darkness in which to hide. For this reason, sometimes the
enveloping darkness in *Scripts* is more sensuously and evocatively
appealing than the light: "*Night, windless, clear. Beneath a crescent moon /
Thousands of little whetted scythes appear / With each slow forward breath of
the great dune*" (168). The image brilliantly evokes the starry gleaming of
the blades of Moslem warriors engaged in a final holy war, a devastating
scenario involving man's ironic destruction of himself through religion.

The minuet of poems for and against man's survival reaches its
conclusion in a vision of the whirling, double-helix shaped DNA
molecule, the symbol and substance of all life. The image is a metaphor-
ical equivalent in *Scripts* for the spinning atom in *Mirabell*. Unlike the
atom, however, it symbolizes the evolution of life in a stable, organized
form, and is thus a hopeful, contemporary version of the shining
primum mobile of Dante's *Paradiso*. The change from atom to DNA
molecule as scientific models of the Dantean vision of heaven is yet
another example of the graduated levels of vision in the trilogy. The
double helix of the DNA molecule is also of course the shape of the
hourglass:

TIME'S MAN BECOME TIME AGAINST MAN:
SAND RUNNING UP, DEEP FUELS TAPPD, MAN
STRADDLING HEAVEN, HEAVEN RECEIVING TIME
WHICH RUNNING OUT THROUGH A MINOAN WAIST
STOPS HERE WHERE WE ARE:
WE WHO (M) LIVING IN THIS RISING DUNE HOLD
IT BACK, HOLD BACK A RESERVOIR OF SPENT TIME,
FEEL AT OUR FEET & LIKEN TO ATOMIC WASTE
THIS WASTE, THIS UPWARD VOLATILE FORCE,
AND KNOW THE TWO SIDES OF MATTER. (193)

The image of the DNA molecule contains most of the important, dialectical motifs of the poem and of the trilogy—heredity versus genetic innovation, death versus survival, erosion versus evolution, resistance versus determinism, matter versus antimatter.

Scripts ends in a masque that sublimates the poem's dialectical motifs into a festive, musical form. The inherited germ of evil and blindness that overshadows the poem enters the dance but in the new, relatively lightly textured form of the "Deceitful *Witch* of the *Black Forest* in the mind" (206). The masque transforms the poem's thoughtful burden into a paean of celebration in which, along with the jubilant figures who now swell the poem, Nature joins: "LET ME CRY A LAST RESOUNDING YES / TO MAN, MAN IN HIS BLESSEDNESS" (207).

The vision tapers off, dissolving at last as Merrill wakes up in Athens to the sound of a barking dog. The ecstatic strains of the masque spill over into the waking world, though, in his response to the night sky:

> Shutter flung wide,
> In streams moonlight, her last quarter blazing
> Inches above that wall of carbon mist
> Made of the neighbors'. Whereupon the bedside
> Tumbler brims and, the tallest story becoming
> Swallowable, a mind-altering spansule,
> This red, self-shuttered poverty and Heaven's
> Glittering oxygen tent as one conspire. (208)

The exquisiteness of these lines delays for a moment the drop from the visionary heights of *Scripts,* but the flow of the poem is that of "diminuendo" and things gradually begin to shrink—rather like the dwindling of Mirabell into the form of a toy peacock in the previous volume. The angels in *Scripts* have also disappeared after the fête although they remain antithetically embedded in the fabric of matter and mind, a fabric that includes Merrill's personal history among other things:

> Between an often absent or abstracted
> (In mid-depression) father and still young
> Mother's wronged air of commonsense the child sat.
> The third and last. If he would never quite
> Outgrow the hobby horse and dragon kite
> Left by the first two, one lukewarm noodle
> Prefigured no less a spiral nebula
> Of further outs. Piano practice, books . . . (213)

The merging of *Scripts*'s cosmological themes with the details of Merrill's youth reflects both the book's integrity and daring. Merrill was his father's third and last child just as man is pictured as nature's third and possibly last creation.

The fusion of self and cosmos in *Scripts for the Pageant* is not simply a final, provocative conceit, but a definitive example of the continuity of mind and matter, here involving the trilogy itself as a universe that evolved out of the self. The poem closes with the breaking of the mirror that had originally enlarged the self's communicative field in the previous volumes of the trilogy. The characters take their farewells on the occasion of David Jackson's birthday amid the visualized background of Venice, which brings the trilogy full circle. As in "The Book of Ephraim" Venice raises the contradictory images of the paradisal and the transitory. The nostalgic, exiled feelings of "The Book of Ephraim" give way here. though, to Merrill's confident acceptance of the present. "Thank Heaven *we're* not twenty," he tells DJ (220).

The curtain falls with the plaintive image of God singing into the universe: "I AND MINE SURVIVE SIGNAL / ME DO YOU WELL I ALONE IN MY NIGHT / HOLD IT BACK HEAR ME BROTHERS I AND MINE" (235). The loneliness that has lain at the bottom of many of Merrill's poems rises her to epic heights. The poem's irony and poignancy derive from the fact that Merrill finds his most engrossing experiences in talking to the dead. The underlying mood of pathos is offset, however, by the prolific inventiveness of the mind, which can people the world—as in the case of the expanded cast at the end of *Scripts*—at the very moment when death appears to have extinguished life and love.

Thus does the principle of "resistance" or "holding back" operate at the deepest emotional level in *Scripts*. Against this background of feeling the poem's cosmology and themes take on the colors of their origins so that their cogency and plausibility are tied to their function as mirrors of the long intimacy of JM and DJ. That intimacy is thus the wheel of light at the poem's center while the epic superstructure resembles the shining mirror of Beatrice's eyes through which Dante first glimpsed the brightness of heaven.

Epilogue

Merrill composed a short epilogue for his trilogy entitled "Birth of the Musician," whose action occurs in the summer of 1978[11] He appended an explanatory note about the epilogue to an excerpt published in the *Harvard Magazine:*

After the third book comes a short epilogue at whose close a reading-aloud of the entire work has been arranged. This will ostensibly take place at the table in our entrance hall in Athens, but no less in the grandly restored ballroom at Sandover, the estate where much of the imagined action goes on. Twenty-six chairs are set up for the likes of Jane Austen, Marius Bewley, Congreve, Dante, Maya Deren—almost an alphabet of august influences and dear ones no longer in the world but vital to the work. Nature has appointed our old friend Ephraim Master of Ceremonies. . . . At the last moment, an empty chair is filled by the all-too-timely death in Rome of Mimí Vassilikos. Her husband, Vassíli, has buried her there, in her favorite white dress, and told us to expect him sooner or later in Athens.[12]

The musician alluded to in the title of the epilogue is Robert Morse, who is to be reborn on a Minnesota farm and who is destined to revolutionize Western music. The action takes place both in the occult "schoolroom" used in *Scripts* and in the womb itself a few days before Morse's birth. In a parallel birth Maria is reborn as a brown-skinned Hindu in Bombay, where her volubility and precociousness as a baby terrify her family. She is destined to become a scientist-premier of India. The rebirth of Maria is especially consoling to JM and DJ (even though it had been forecast at the end of *Scripts*) because it appears to override her earlier fate of being destined to become a plant. Both destinies in fact come to pass in the trilogy.

The choice of Morse to do V work is particularly fortuitous since his previous life had been so desultory and unproductive. In honor of the change that has overtaken him Merrill describes Morse's birth as if it were the Nativity, recalling poems like "Verse for Urania" and "Chimes for Yahya" from *Divine Comedies* and thus bringing the trilogy full circle in this respect as well. Morse, sleeping peacefully *in utero,* is visited by angels who, like the wise men in the Nativity story, bring gifts—here the priceless gifts of the five senses. With the gift of sight Morse discovers with dismay that he will be crippled in one foot. The affliction, he is made to understand, will force him to concentrate on his work for mankind instead of dissipating his energies as he had done in his previous existence: "HOBBLED YOU WILL LEAP". As the embryological development of the new Robert Morse proceeds, the features of the old Morse fade, a tender sign that Merrill and Jackson have finally accepted the death of their friend.

The epilogue concludes within a tiered setting—Athens and Sandover—the latter being the heavenly estate built to accommodate the cast of Merrill's trilogy. A midsummer pageant is to be performed. The pervasive atmosphere of Shakespeare's *Midsummer Night's Dream* is particularly visible in the motif of unmasking. Ephraim is suddenly revealed as Michael in disguise, thereby revising the relationship between "The Book of Ephraim" and *Scripts for the Pageant* and redefining hell allegorically as simply a narrow view of heaven. Nature as Queen Mum restates the purpose of the revelations vouchsafed to JM and DJ: "REVELATION'S CONSTANT PROCESS CANNOT BE TRUSTED TO THE HACK / JOURNALIST: EXTRA! EXTRA! GOD SURVIVES! / RATHER, ON A TUSCAN HILLSIDE A SIMPLE MENDICANT BEGINS: T H E R E   A R E   N I N E   S T A-G E S." Following Dante's lead, Merrill reaffirms the divinity of the world not through statement but through the allurements of narrative, which, unlike statement, induces belief.

"The Ballroom at Sandover" draws the poem's cast together for a final reading of the poem, and the ambience is sumptuously elegant for the occasion:

High ceiling where a faun-Pythagoras
Loses his calipers to barefoot, faintly
Goitrous nymphs, nor pier-glasses between
Floral panels of the palest green . . .
chandeliers aclick like chaperones
Indulgently at crystals one by one
Accenting the donnée sun-beamed through tall
French window, silver leaf and waxing bud,
All a felicity.

As Merrill takes in the room, he becomes gradually aware that it is familiar, that it is in fact the gilded room of his youth, the "old ballroom of the Broken Home." The recently dead Mimí Vassilikos enters dressed in white and slightly dazed at first, but she soon takes her place with the assembled guests, who in a festive mood await the beginning of the reading. The scene seals the trilogy and at the same time consummates all of Merrill's previous writings. The setting of his unhappy youth, revisited in earlier, melancholy poems, here becomes the very chamber of heaven. The metamorphosis epitomizes the structure of Merrill's divine comedies, which convert the autobiographical strands of an all too vulnerable life into the stuff of epic.

Chapter Seven

A Final Reckoning

In his prize-winning story, "The English Gardens" (1961), David Jackson created a character named "Meredith" who bears a remarkable resemblance to James Merrill:

For every critic who called his poetry too often shallow and mocking, there were three who protested that he had managed the hardest of all things: to speak lightly of tragic affairs. Through all of this he pursued his own way. Unlike Paul Klee's defiant, "To hell with uncle, let's get on with our building," Meredith's pun, "I can only fly where I fly—and so the shallows always come back to Capistrano," hid his fear that, perhaps, those severer critics were right.[1]

Merrill's quiet resolve to go his own way was finally recognized by the judges of the National Book Award for poetry in 1967. The judges, who that year included W. H. Auden, Howard Nemerov, and James Dickey, lauded Merrill for his "scrupulous and uncompromising cultivation of the poetic art, evidenced in his refusal to settle for an easy and profitable stance; for his insistence on taking the kind of tough, poetic chances which make the difference between aesthetic success or failure."[2] High praise for a poet who up to that point had often been written about as one of the "elegants" who "promised most and delivered least," as James Dickey had put it in a review of *The Country of a Thousand Years of Peace* in 1959.[3]

A problem surrounding the early reception of Merrill's work was that he simply did not fit. He seemed to belong with Confessional poets like Robert Lowell and John Berryman, and yet he was different. In Merrill, as in the writing of Elizabeth Bishop whose work he much admires, the personal experience that forms the basis of the poetry does not give rise to feelings of self-alienation as happens in Berryman and Lowell. In addition, his aloofness from social issues amounted to a mild rebuke of the social commitment felt by many American poets and critics in the 1950s and 1960s. His aloofness was based in part upon his belief that

146

society as a poetic subject would have been a flat substitute indeed for the depth and subtlety that are discoverable within an individual human life. Consequently, in his trilogy of divine comedies he portrays collective man as shaped by a few extraordinary individuals who are perceived to be the leaven of history and civilization. For Merrill, as for Proust, the self was the measure of all things, and by the time he had written *Scripts for the Pageant* in 1980 there would be nothing of importance that the self in his writings had not already assimilated; microcosm had become macrocosm.

In retrospect, Merrill's writings seem all of a piece. He conflated his early experience with plays and novels, for example, into the dramatic and narrative poems of the 1960s and 1970s. In addition, the central theme of all of this work has been more or less constant throughout Merrill's life—the cumulative pleasures of consciousness against the slippage of loneliness and aging. The pursuit of this theme has seemed to some to be evidence of Merrill's essential elitism. Certainly, critics of the early work regretted its profound detachment and apparent devotion to the decorative. Merrill's tacit reply, incorporated in his writings during the 1950s and early 1960s, was to center himself on that which, for better or worse, constituted his experience. In the earliest poems that experience is primarily aesthetic, engrossing enough in its way if also somewhat coolly distant. Gradually, he overcame the unsettled, self-conscious feelings about his childhood, family breakup, and emergent homosexuality, and ventured into an autobiographical art— beginning with *The Country of a Thousand Years of Peace*—that clearly sprang from something deep within him.

In spite of Merrill's refined handling of complex, epistemological themes in his early work and the impressive comprehensiveness of his grasp of intellectual history in the divine comedies, he is not primarily a philosophical poet. He was interested in ideas chiefly as sources through which to portray the color and movement of consciousness. For Merrill it is the gratuitous play of the mind that is the surest sign of its value in a world that otherwise seems shadowed by calculation and acquisitiveness. The mind at play is also what underlies his use of poetic form. The flexible rhymes, the adaptations of traditional, sometimes esoteric stanzas to contemporary, conversational rhythms, and the profuse crystallizing of images out of the thinnest air all mirror the play of mind. It is especially through Merrill's prolific use of form, reflecting the applied heat of one of the foremost poetic craftsmen of the postwar period, that he is able to illuminate the hidden significance of an otherwise uneventful life.

In some respects, rather than being an elitist, Merrill is the most egalitarian of writers since he extended the reach of American poetry into the most mundane recesses of everyday life. Nowhere has his success been more apparent than in the innovatively designed and richly textured autobiographical studies that extend throughout the middle period of his career from *Water Street* to the shorter poems in *Divine Comedies*. Moreover, in contrast to his early reserve, he reaches a new level of candor in the trilogy of divine comedies that in some respects surpasses even that of the Confessional poets. He does so because he reveals not only intensely personal aspects of his emotional and sexual life but, in addition, exposes the vulnerable tenuousness and uncertainty of his mind as it voyages into new fields of poetic consciousness. He is sympathetic to those who have gagged on "The Book of Ephraim," *Mirabell,* and *Scripts for the Pageant* because of the bizarre nature of some of the motifs found therein. Indeed, he has had such feelings himself.

Nevertheless, at its deeper levels Merrill's trilogy represents a disarming, original, and sophisticated assault against some key assumptions underlying modern culture. The fables of his divine comedies with their mixture of mythology, erudition, domesticity, and luxuriant language not only reflect the workings of a powerful imagination, but also capture the unsettling ambiguity of the mind's simultaneously advanced and atavistic makeup. The pattern had emerged from Merrill's study of his own psyche in the poems of the 1950s and 1960s with their perceptual montages of frightened, lonely child and adrift adult, each claiming to represent the real James Merrill. Looked at in this light, Merrill's divine comedies can be seen as a comprehensive, imaginative synthesis in which vivid narrative archetypes depict the restless, overlapping, historical flow of consciousness from one existential dimension to another—from infant to adult, from individual to tribe or state, from primitive savage to modern cosmopolite, from sage to fetus, from animal to angel.

With steady attention to his task, Merrill finally opposes his model of mind and culture to the simplified literalism which he perceives contemporary culture as mistaking for reality. The problem with literalism, Merrill implicitly argues through his work, is that it tends to undervalue and thereby to imperil the life process. This is why he worked so strenuously in *Braving the Elements, Divine Comedies, Mirabell,* and *Scripts for the Pageant* to divinize the forms of life down to the most minute and homely chemical compounds. In this way his argument for the usefulness of the artist in a scientific age becomes apparent—fanciful child though the artist may at times appear to be. Without this *particular* child, Merrill insistently suggests, there will be no others. Merrill thus turns out—however self-consciously—to be a visionary poet of some magnitude and to have thereby carved for himself a rare and distinctive place in recent American writing.

Notes and References

Chapter One

1. Unpublished, undated biographical sketch. Merrill Collection, Washington University, St. Louis.

2. Interview with the author June 13, 1980. Part of this interview has been published in the *Arizona Quarterly* (Spring, 1982).

3. Ashley Brown, "An Interview with James Merrill," *Shenandoah* 19 (Summer 1968):5. Subsequently identified as Brown interview.

4. Unpublished manuscript, dated November 13, 1948. Notebook B, Merrill Collection, Washington University, St. Louis.

5. Brown interview, p. 3.

6. Interview with the author, June 13, 1980.

7. Ibid.

8. Unpublished manuscript. Merrill Collection, Washington University, St. Louis.

9. *Mirabell: Books of Number* (New York, 1980). Page references appear in the text.

10. David Kalstone, "The Poet: Private," *Saturday Review,* December 2, 1972, p. 44. Subsequently identified as the Kalstone interview.

11. Brown interview, 4.

12. Statement at the National Book Award Presentation Ceremonies in New York, March 8, 1967. Manuscript. Merrill Collection, Washington University, St. Louis.

13. Brown interview, pp. 11–12.

14. Interview with the author, June 13, 1980.

15. James Merrill, "Marvellous Poet," *New York Review of Books,* July 17, 1975, p. 14.

16. Robert K. Martin, *The Homosexual Tradition in American Poetry* (Austin, Texas, and London, 1979), p. 191.

17. Merrill, "Marvellous Poet," p. 15.

18. Interview with the author, June 13, 1980.

19. Ibid.

20. Donald Sheehan, "An Interview with James Merrill," *Contemporary Literature* 9 (1968):3. Subsequently identified as Sheehan interview.

21. Letter to the author, June 2, 1980.

22. Brown interview, p. 7.

23. Interview with the author, June 13, 1980.

24. Sheehan interview, p. 3.

25. Brown interview, p. 9.

26. Interview with the author, June 13, 1980.

27. Sheehan interview, 13.

28. Unpublished manuscript. Merrill Collection, Washington University, St. Louis.

29. Manuscript. Notebook M (1964). Merrill Collection, Washington University, St. Louis.

30. Manuscript. Notebook D (1950–51). Merrill Collection, Washington University, St. Louis.

31. James Merrill, *Scripts for the Pageant* (New York, 1980), p. 137. Page references appear in the text.

32. James Merrill, *Divine Comedies* (New York, 1976). Page references appear in the text.

33. T. S. Eliot, "Henry James," in *Selected Prose of T. S. Eliot,* ed. Frank Kermode (New York: Harcourt, Brace Jovanovich / Farrar Straus & Giroux, 1975), p. 152.

34. Sheehan interview, p. 10.

35. James Merrill, "Object Lessons," *New York Review of Books,* November 30, 1972, p. 31.

36. Ibid.

37. Ibid.

38. Brown interview, p. 6.

39. Sheehan interview, p. 10.

40. Ibid.

41. Ibid., p. 11.

42. Interview with the author, June 13, 1980.

43. Merrill, "Object Lessons," p. 34.

44. Sheehan interview, p. 5.

45. Ibid., p. 3.

46. Merrill, "Marvellous Poet," p. 14.

47. Kalstone interview, p. 45.

48. Unpublished manuscript. Merrill Collection, Washington University, St. Louis.

49. Kalstone interview, p. 45.

50. Sheehan interview, p. 6.

51. Ibid., p. 7.

52. Ibid., p. 8.

53. James Merrill, "Notes on Corot," in *Corot 1796–1875: An Exhibition of His Paintings and Graphic Works* (Chicago, 1960), p. 11.

54. Sheehan interview, p. 5.

55. James Merrill, "Robert Bagg: A Postscript," *Poetry* 98 (1961):252.

56. Anon., "Interview with James Merrill," *Stage Four* (privately printed, 1969), pp. 47–48.

57. Ibid., p. 47.

58. Ibid.

59. Kalstone interview, p. 45.

60. Ibid.

61. James Merrill, "A *la Recherche du Temps Perdu*: Impressionism in Literature." Manuscript. All quotations in the next four paragraphs (to the end of Section V) are from this unpublished manuscript source, which is located in the Merrill Collection, Washington University, St. Louis.

62. Interview with the author, June 13, 1980.

63. Merrill, "Marvellous Poet," p. 16.

64. Sheehan interview, pp. 13, 8.

65. James Merrill, *The Country of a Thousand Years of Peace* (New York, 1958). Page references appear in the text.

66. Merrill, "Object Lessons," p. 33.

67. *Stage Four* interview, p. 48.

68. Sheehan interview, p. 2.

69. *Stage Four* interview, p. 47.

70. Quotations from "Object Lessons," p. 32.

71. Sheehan interview, p. 3.

72. James Merrill, "Elizabeth Bishop (1911–1979)," *New York Review of Books,* December 6, 1979, p. 6.

73. Sheehan interview, p. 6.

74. Brown interview, p. 15.

Chapter Two

1. Helen Vendler, "James Merrill's Myth: An Interview," *New York Review of Books,* May 3, 1979, p. 12. Subsequently identified as the Vendler interview.

2. James Merrill, "The Bait," in *Artists' Theatre: Four Plays,* ed. Herbert Machiz (New York and London, 1960). Page references appear in the text.

3. Interview with the author, June 13, 1980.

4. Brown interview, p. 11.

5. Interview with the author, June 13, 1980.

6. James Merrill, "The Immortal Husband," in *Playbook: Five Plays for a New Theatre* (New York, 1956). Page references appear in the text.

Chapter Three

1. Sheehan interview, p. 4.

2. James Merrill, "Driver," *Partisan Review* 29 (1962):491–506. Page references appear in the text. The story was later collected in Howard Moss's *The Poet's Story* (New York: Macmillan, 1973).

3. James Merrill, "Peru: The Landscape Game," *Prose,* Spring 1971, pp. 105–14. Page references appear in the text.

4. James Merrill, *The Seraglio* (New York, 1957). Page references appear in the text.

5. Manuscript. Notes for *The (Diblos) Notebook,* October 5, 1962. Merrill Collection, Washington University, St. Louis.

6. Ibid.

7. Ibid.

8. Ibid.

9. Manuscript. Notes for *The (Diblos) Notebook,* June 27, 1961. Merrill Collection, Washington University, St. Louis.

10. James Merrill, *The (Diblos) Notebook* (New York, 1965). Page references appear in the text.

11. Manuscript. Notes for *The (Diblos) Notebook,* October 5, 1962. Merrill Collection, Washington University, St. Louis.

12. Ibid., October 4, 1962.

13. Interview with the author, June 13, 1980.

14. Brown interview, p. 11.

Chapter Four

1. James Merrill, *The Black Swan* (Athens, 1946). Page references appear in the text.

2. Howard Nemerov, *Poetry and Fiction* (New Brunswick, N.J.: Rutgers University Press, 1963), p. 195.

3. James Merrill, *First Poems* (New York, 1951). Page references appear in the text.

4. Interview with the author, June 13, 1980.

5. Brown interview, p. 9.

6. Ibid., p. 10.

7. James Merrill, *Short Stories* (Pawlet, Vt., 1954). Page references appear in the text.

8. Brown interview, p. 10.

9. Ibid.

Chapter Five

1. James Merrill, *Water Street* (New York, 1962). Page references appear in the text.

2. Letter to the author, November 21, 1980.

3. Brown interview, p. 9.

4. James Merrill, *Nights and Days* (New York, 1966). Page references appear in the text.

5. Brown interview, p. 14.

6. Sheehan interview, p. 8.

7. Interview with the author, June 13, 1980.

8. Sheehan interview, p. 8.

9. James Merrill, *The Fire Screen* (New York, 1969). Page references appear in the text.

10. Merrill, "Marvellous Poet," p. 14.

11. Interview with the author, June 13, 1980.

12. James Merrill, *Braving the Elements* (New York, 1972). Page references appear in the text.

13. Letter to the author, September 27, 1980.

14. Interview with the author, June 13, 1980.

15. James Merrill, *The Yellow Pages* (Cambridge, Mass., 1974). Page references appear in the text.

Chapter Six

1. Kalstone interview, p. 45.

2. Interview with the author, June 13, 1980.

3. Ibid.

4. Ibid.

5. Vendler interview, p. 12.

6. Ibid.

7. "Note" by James Merrill in *Kenyon Review,* n.s. 1 (Summer 1979):158.

8. Vendler interview, p. 12.

9. Interview with the author, June 13, 1980.

10. See Isaac Asimov, *Asimov's Guide to Science* (New York: Basic Books, 1972), p. 311.

11. At the time of this writing, the epilogue is scheduled to be published in *The Changing Light at Sandover,* volume two of Merrill's selected poems, which is being brought out by Atheneum. Quotations are from a photoduplicated copy of 25 pages with which Merrill has supplied the author.

12. James Merrill, "The Ballroom at Sandover," *Harvard Magazine,* September–October 1980, p. 38.

Chapter Seven

1. David Jackson, "The English Gardens," in *Prize Stories 1962: The O. Henry Awards,* ed. Richard Poirier (New York: Doubleday, 1962), p. 162. Originally published in *Partisan Review,* Spring, 1961, 201–44.

2. Manuscript. Citation of the Judges of the National Book Award in Poetry for James Merrill's *Nights and Days,* 1967. Merrill Collection, Washington University, St. Louis.

3. The review has been reprinted in James Dickey's *Babel to Byzantium: Poets & Poetry Now* (New York, 1968), p. 97.

Selected Bibliography

PRIMARY SOURCES

1. Poems

The Black Swan. Athens: Icaros, 1946.

Braving the Elements. New York: Atheneum, 1972.

The Country of a Thousand Years of Peace. New York: Knopf, 1959.

Divine Comedies. New York: Atheneum, 1976.

The Fire Screen. New York: Atheneum, 1969.

First Poems. New York: Knopf, 1951.

Jim's Book: A Collection of Poems and Short Stories. New York: privately printed, 1942.

Mirabell: Books of Number. New York: Atheneum, 1978.

Nights and Days. New York: Atheneum, 1966.

Scripts for the Pageant. New York: Atheneum, 1980.

Short Stories. Pawlet, Vt.: Banyan Press, 1954.

Water Street. New York: Atheneum, 1962.

The Yellow Pages. Cambridge, Mass.: Temple Bar Bookshop, 1974.

2. Novels

The (Diblos) Notebook. New York: Atheneum, 1965.

The Seraglio. New York: Knopf, 1957.

3. Plays

The Bait. Published in *Artists' Theatre: Four Plays.* Edited by Herbert Machiz. New York: Grove Press, 1960.

The Immortal Husband. Published in *Playbook: Plays for a New Theatre.* New York: New Directions, 1956.

4. Short Stories

"Driver." *Partisan Review* 29 (1962):491–506.

"Peru: The Landscape Game." *Prose,* Spring 1971, pp. 105–14.

5. Essays

"Foreword." *La Sorelle Bronte* by Bernard de Zagheb. New York: Tibor de
    Nagy, 1963.

"Notes on Corot." *Corot 1796–1875: An Exhibition of His Paintings and
    Graphic Works.* Chicago: Art Institute of Chicago, 1960, pp. 11–15.

6. Articles

"Divine Poem." *New Republic,* November 29, 1980, pp. 29–34.

"Elizabeth Bishop (1911–1979)." *New York Review of Books,* December 6,
    1979, p. 6.

"Marvellous Poet." *New York Review of Books,* July 17, 1975, pp. 12–17.

"Object Lessons." *New York Review of Books,* November 30, 1972, pp.
    31–33.

"The Relic, Promises, and Poems." *Voices,* no. 166 (May–August
    1958):47–55.

"Robert Bagg: A Postscript." *Poetry* 98 (July 1961):250–52.

SECONDARY SOURCES

1. Books

Dickey, James. *Babel to Byzantium: Poets and Poetry Now.* New York: Farrar,
    Straus, & Giroux, 1968, pp. 97–100. Reprint of Dickey's 1968 review
    of *The Country of a Thousand Years of Peace,* a review that Merrill told the
    author he had found helpful.

Howard, Richard. *Alone With America.* New York: Atheneum, 1969, pp.
    327–48. Sensitive assessment of Merrill's work by a poet of some note
    himself.

Kalstone, David. *Five Temperaments: Elizabeth Bishop, Robert Lowell, James
    Merrill, Adrienne Rich, John Ashbery.* New York: Oxford University
    Press, 1977, pp. 77–128. An astute overview of Merrill's writings.

Martin, Robert K. *The Homosexual Tradition in American Poetry.* Austin and
    London: University of Texas Press, 1979. Useful introduction to con-
    ventions used in modern poetry by homosexuals in general and Merrill
    in particular.

Vendler, Helen. *Part of Nature, Part of Us: Modern American Poets.* Cam-
    bridge, Mass.: Harvard University Press, 1980, pp. 205–32. Reprint
    of influential reviews of *Braving the Elements, Divine Comedies,* and
    Mirabell.

2. Articles

Bromwich, David. "Answer Heavenly Muse, Yes or No." *Hudson Review* 32 (1979):455–60. Concise assessment of Merrill's development from autobiography to epic.

Eaves, Maurice. "Decision and Revision in James Merrill's *(Diblos) Notebook.*" *Contemporary Literature* 12 (1971):156–65. Helpful introduction to a difficult book.

Ettin, Andrew V. "On James Merrill's 'Nights and Days.' " *Perspective* 15 (1967):33–51. One of the first lengthy discussions of Merrill's poetry.

Hallberg, Robert von. "James Merrill: 'Revealing By Obscuring.' " *Contemporary Literature* 21 (1980):549–71. Interesting analysis of Merrill's periphrastic method.

Moffatt, Judith. "Masked More and Less Than Ever: James Merrill's *Braving the Elements.*" *Hollins Critic* 10 (June 1973):1–10. Persuasive discussion of Merrill as a hermetic poet.

————. "The Other World and the Real." *Poetry* 129 (1976):40–53. Fruitful analysis of the poems in *Divine Comedies.*

Park, Clara Claiborne. "Where 'The Waste Land' Ends." *Nation* 230 (May 3, 1980):532–35. Perceptive analysis of *Scripts for the Pageant.*

Saez, Richard. "James Merrill's Oedipal Fire." *Parnassus* 3, no. 1 (1974):159–84. Thoughtful exploration of the Oedipal motif in Merrill's poems, centering on *Braving the Elements* and *The Yellow Pages.*

Sloss, Henry. "James Merrill's *The Book of Ephraim.*" *Shenandoah* 27, no. 4 (1976):63–91; 28, no. 1 (1976):83–110. A two-part meticulous analysis of the structure of "The Book of Ephraim."

Spender, Stephen. "Heaven Can't Wait." *New York Review of Books,* December 21, 1978, pp. 34–36. A lively, tough-minded appraisal of *Mirabell.*

Yenser, Stephen. "Feux D'Artifice." *Poetry* 122 (1973):163–68. An incisive analysis of the imagery of fire in Merrill's poetry, particularly in *Braving the Elements.*

3. Interviews

Anon. "Interview with James Merrill." *Stage Four.* New York: privately printed, 1969, pp. 46–48. A brief but illuminating interview published, according to Merrill, by a private-school coop in New York and New England. Difficult to find, but included among Merrill's papers at Washington University in St. Louis.

Brown, Ashley. "An Interview with James Merrill." *Shenandoah* 19, no. 4 (1968):3–15. An indispensable source of information about many aspects of Merrill's art.

Kalstone, David. "The Poet: Private." *Saturday Review,* December 2, 1972, pp. 43–45. Excellent source of information about "Yánnina."

Labrie, Ross. "James Merrill at Home: An Interview." *Arizona Quarterly* 38 (1982): 19–36. Covers the whole range of Merrill's work up to and including *Scripts for the Pageant.*

Sheehan, Donald. "An Interview with James Merrill." *Contemporary Literature* 9 (1968): 1–14. Contains valuable material on Merrill's plays and novels as well as his poems.

Vendler, Helen. "James Merrill's Myth: An Overview." *New York Review of Books,* May 3, 1979, pp. 12–13. Valuable source of information about *Mirabell* and the divine comedies in general.

Index